WOMEN'S VOICES
FROM THE OREGON TRAIL

WOMEN'S VOICES
FROM THE OREGON TRAIL
The Times That Tried Women's Souls
and
A Guide to Women's History
Along the Oregon Trail

by
Susan G. Butruille

Artwork by Kathleen Petersen
Photographs by Author unless otherwise noted

tamarack books inc.

First edition, January, 1993
Second edition, March, 1993

PUBLISHED BY:
Tamarack Books, Inc.
PO Box 190313
Boise, ID 83719-0313

COVER AND BOOK DESIGN BY:
Kathleen Petersen

TYPESETTING BY:
Typography by Gail Ward
124 S 5th
Boise, Idaho 83702

Permission to quote graciously granted from Yale University Press for: Faragher, John Mack. *Women and Men on the Overland Trail.* New Haven and London: Yale University Press, 1979.

About the cover: The background is a photograph of a portion of an 1850 friendship quilt called Album Patch, from the collection of Pat Ferrero, author of *Hearts and Hands: The Influence of Women and Quilts on American Society.* Made of blocks signed by sixteen friends and relatives, it represents the treasured quilts women took with them across the Oregon Trail. (Courtesy of Hearts and Hands Media Arts)

The "Pioneer Woman" statue, sculpted by Juan Lombardo, stands in the landscape garden of the National Frontier Trails Center in Independence, Missouri. Facing west, the determined young mother represents the pioneer spirit of the women who were part of the westward movement.

AUTHOR'S NOTE:
The recipes printed in this book are intended for reading only, not necessarily for eating. I take no responsibility for any food prepared according to these "receipts."

DEDICATION

To my mother, Ruth Hendricks Greffenius, who blazed the trail for me.

And
To the men in my life:
John, my best friend and partner
Our sons, Frank and Tony

And the memory of my father, R. J. Greffenius.

To the women on the Trail
whose voices speak of persistence
To the women who were here before
whose voices plead for community

Special thanks to:
Lillian Schlissel, whose friendship I have come to treasure as much as her eloquence; William Bullard, whose Trail expertise and encouragement kept me going; Linda Burt, Kathy Jones, Deborah Olsen, George Olsen, Victoria Shenk, Judy Mann DiStefano (in memoriam), Alice Armstrong, Paula McKenzie, Mary Alice Kier, Richard E. Greffenius, Barbara Greffenius, and especially my publisher-turned-friend, Kathy Gaudry.

CONTENTS

Part I

WOMEN'S VOICES FROM THE OREGON TRAIL

The Times That Tried Women's Souls

PRELUDE

As I traveled, I kept meeting myself on the trail.

Some thought they were brave. Some—like Horace Greeley (contrary to popular belief)—said they were nuts: those people who traveled more than 2,000 miles across prairie and sage, mountains and valleys and rivers and God only knew what else, in search of—what? Free land. Free-dom. Better health. Adventure. Themselves. Some went because they couldn't not go. Others went because they couldn't say no. Those in that last category were women.

The one thing that united them was hope. Hope for something better than what they had.

The 1843 trek from Independence, Missouri to Oregon Country became known as the Great Migration, the first of many that would open new Western frontiers and change the course of American history. Oregon Trail migrations continued through the 1840s, peaked in the 1850s, and mingled with other westward migrations in the 1860s as lands between the Missouri River and the West Coast opened to settlement. With the Oregon Trail 150th birthday commemoration coming up in 1993, I wanted to be in on the celebration.

As a fifteen-year teacher, student, writer and speaker on women's history, I thought it would be fun to trace the trail, learn more about it, and track down and write about places of interest about women: landmarks, statues, signposts, markers, grave stones—anything that helps keep women's stories alive along the Oregon Trail. I'd done that in Washington, D.C. and in Oregon. Why not the Oregon Trail?

So I did what any independent-minded woman with a mission would do. I called my mother. I asked her to fly from Colorado and meet me in Independence, Missouri, and explore the Oregon Trail with me back to my home in Oregon. Of course she would, she said. She wouldn't miss it.

On a sunny Saturday morning I hugged my husband, said a teary good-bye and headed for Independence. This was an adventure I had wanted to share with John. I would be exploring some of the country he loved most, especially in the stark sage country of Wyoming. Still, I've always enjoyed exploring by myself—making my own decisions and having time to think and observe. I'd be alone until I got to Independence. I watched through the rear view mirror as John walked away without turning back to wave. He never has liked good-byes.

It was October, not the usual misty Oregon October. This day was warm and sunny. It was a splendid time to be driving Oregon's cliff-lined, gold-tinged Columbia River Gorge, where dams have calmed the waters since the emigrants made their terrifying trip headlong down the Columbia River's furious waters.

My life and travels with John have taken us to some spectacular places in the West—the inside passage of Southeast Alaska, the Grand Tetons and Yellowstone Park of Wyoming, and the Rocky Mountains of Colorado, where I grew up. The Columbia River Gorge, which forms the border between Washington and Oregon, remains my favorite place. Its moods and grandeur captivate me, and each visit reveals a new waterfall or rivulet that had hidden from me before.

Columbia River

On this day, though, the gorge was in an unfriendly mood. Angry clouds filled the sky above Multnomah Falls. As I sped by, I saw orange flames climbing the mountain dangerously close to the historic Multnomah Falls Lodge. Helicopters hovered near the flames. I would learn later that fire damage would close the trail above the lodge, which itself remained untouched.

This was about the time of year the first emigrants would be approaching the most dangerous part of the trip. Their greatest danger would be not fire, but water. They would cross the treacherous Blue Mountains of what is now Eastern Oregon and then convert their wagons to rafts—if indeed they had any wagons left—and float them down the raging Columbia River to the promised land of the Willamette Valley.

That night, in a Boise motel room, I wrote in my journal: *I can't escape the contrast. Today I drove in less than a day the entire distance that was the most dangerous part of the Oregon Trail. I still can't conceive of their hardship any more than they could imagine me doing what I did today.*

As I traveled, I listened to a tape of Lillian Schlissel's 1982 book *Women's Diaries of the Westward Journey*. What a backdrop for the women's voices: seeing through my windshield the country they trudged through for five, six, even eight months, unprotected from weather and sickness.

The expressive voice reading the book described women's ties to family, home and community, and their sorrow at leaving, to take this journey across the unknown.

> **I am going with him, as there is no
> other alternative.**[1]
> —Margaret Hereford Wilson, 1850

Schlissel reminds us that most men who headed west were in their physical prime, ready for adventure. For most women, the journey came during the most vulnerable time of their lives— their childbearing years.

Now, imagine a young farm wife and mother whose husband announces that he has sold the farm, and they are to start preparing for the 2,000 mile trek to Oregon. The family has probably moved from farther east at least once before, but this is home. It's settled. Her family and friends are here. Her whole being is connected with this house, this community. If she leaves this place, who is she?

Some women readily agreed to go. Many did not. Legally, it didn't matter what the wife thought, because nineteenth-century law gave the husband the right to decide where the family lived. If that was 2,000 miles across an unknown land, that's where it would be.

I listened as women's diaries recorded the pain of leaving. Counting the miles by the graves of cholera and accident victims. Burying the dead and then driving the wagons over the grave to hide the body from wolves and Indians. The stench of animal carcasses along the alkali water country of Wyoming. Skull-deadening boredom. The heart-break of separation on the trail as families either lost track of one another or chose to go separate ways. Struggling to keep some semblance of "civilization" on the trail against the uncivilizing intrusions of dust and mud and water and bugs and blood and vomit. Facing starvation after following bad advice to take an untried cutoff. Children falling from wagons. Husbands drowning in river crossings or dying from accidental gunshot wounds. Giving birth on the trail and relying on the comfort and help of other women. Struggling to keep from giving in to emotions, fearing insanity. At the end of the journey, the woman's recognition that she would never again be the same person who left her home many months and miles ago.

The words of Elizabeth Stewart Warner describing her 1853 journey seemed to capture women's experience for me. After witnessing death from drowning and sickness, becoming separated from a sister who was traveling with her, and watching oxen die one by one, Elizabeth and her party took an untried cutoff:

> **. . . then we came to the new road**
> **they talk about the times that tried men**
> **souls but if this ware not the times that**
> **tried both men and wemon's souls . . .**

Along with the women's voices from the book, I listened to Seattle songwriter Linda Allen's music. Especially fitting was "Overland 1852," a song inspired by stories from *Women's Diaries of the Westward Journey.*

My name is Emma Logan and I come
  from Tennessee
And there I spent my childhood with
  my friends and family.
I married young John Logan back in
  1844.
That day he promised Pa we'd never go
  far from his door.

The children came so quickly, but my
  ma was so close by.
She'd help out with the births and then
  she'd hold 'em when they'd cry.
I thought my life was settled 'til the day
  John said to me,
'Pack the wagon, woman, we are
  leaving Tennessee.'
—from "Overland 1852"
©1982, Linda Allen

Despite misgivings about the journey, many women began their diaries in optimism. Many ended in despair. At the start of her 1845 Oregon Trail trek, Miriam Thompson Tuller wrote of her husband's patriotism and her own "spirit of adventure and a desire to see what was new and strange."

In October rain and mud, she made the final leg of the journey on foot and horseback around Mount Hood into the Willamette Valley. Still trying to remain optimistic, she wrote:

[W]hen I saw a woman on a very
poor horse with a little child in her lap
and one strapped on behind her and
two or three tied on another horse, I
felt thankful and imagined I was only
having a picnic.[2]

The women's voices spun around in my head as the landscape unfolded. Along with the diaries and Linda Allen's songs, I listened to other recordings. The poignant melody of Rodrigo's *Concierto de Aranjuez* seemed fitting as the hot, dry Wyoming vistas stretched before me. Some Italian arias. Jazz by Marian McPartland. The landscape turned from the Wyoming sage prairies to the wide waters of the Platte River in Nebraska to the grass and wheat of the Kansas hills.

Within five days, I was at the Kansas City airport picking up my mother, Ruth Greffenius. The new friends she had made on the flight had already heard about our upcoming adventure. It was comforting to see Mother there, to know that she would make this journey with me. On the trail, I would introduce her as my colleague, Ruth, for she was that. It seemed unprofessional to be calling my colleague Mother. That evening, Ruth and I enjoyed a sort of celebration dinner, and toasted what lay ahead.

That night—our first official night "on the trail"—I lay awake, listened to the faint sounds of traffic outside, and the persistent thudding of my heart. I knew where I was going. I knew my final destination. I knew that awaiting me at the end of the journey were the strong arms of my husband and a cozy home.

Yet the fears tugged at me. I was to speak at a conference in less than two weeks. *What if the car breaks down and I don't get back in time? What if we get caught in an early storm crossing those endless stretches of lonely Wyoming highways? What if I somehow mess up the thirty rolls of film I've packed? What if Mother gets sick? What if I get sick? And who do I think I am anyway—coming all this way, spending all this money to write this book that's now just a dream?*

As I lay awake, I began to hear again the faint voices and the wrenching fears of the women poised on the edge of that same distance a century and a half ago. It would take Mother and me twelve days to drive back home in the safety and comfort of a contraption those women would not even have imagined. They believed it would be a difficult trip of perhaps three or four months. More likely, it would be a six-month trail of heartbreak.

A woman lies awake in a tent on the outskirts of Independence. After traveling down the Missouri on a steamboat with their belongings, she and her husband and children have spent several weeks in this muddy tent city making final preparations and joining up with a wagon train. They have stored additional supplies and bought and bartered for the oxen, horses, cows and chickens that would haul and sustain them on the journey ahead. Others around her have traveled in their wagons all the way from home.

The woman has left her home and all she has known hundreds of miles away. Now it is early May, and the men are arguing over whether or not the grass is tall enough for the oxen to find enough to eat. The decision is to leave tomorrow.

Packed in a trunk in the wagon beside the tent are her most precious belongings. A few pieces of china. A Bible. Matches. Medicines. A flatiron her mother has given her. A linen table cloth. Napkins. Remembrances of sisters and brothers, friends, perhaps parents she has left behind. And a friendship quilt presented to her before she left. Friends embroidered their names, with sayings like "remember me" on separate blocks, then joined them together for warmth and comfort and remembering in the miles ahead.

She hears her husband nearing the tent. His unsteady voice reveals that he has spent a final night at a local grog shop, celebrating the upcoming adventure. She wonders how he'll handle the unfamiliar job of managing the oxen and the other livestock, especially if he is still feeling the alcohol. Her imagination races beyond the first uncertain miles of the journey to places unknown. What do they hold? Riches? Sickness? Separation? Death?

Night surrounds her. She hears the milling of cattle and oxen hooves in their penned-up restlessness. She never has gotten used to the acrid odor of the livestock pens. A child whimpers beside her in restless slumber as his brothers and sisters lie asleep, tucked in crowded bundles.

Perhaps the woman hears the faint sound of her own voice as she tries to hide her longing for her mother, friends, sisters left behind.

My mother sleeps in the bed beside mine. I can't imagine leaving her, looking back and seeing her there, knowing I will never see her again. Just months before, Mother and I looked on my dad's worn face for the last time. I am still lonely for him as my thoughts race backward and forward in time.

I know the sound of a woman's voice—my own—as a wail involuntarily escapes her, realizing she has seen the face and heard the voice of a beloved friend for the last time.

The words of a woman who crossed the Oregon Trail in 1852 echo in my tired brain: "O my heart yearns for thee my only friend. . . . I will never forget thee the earliest friend . . . I know I can never enjoy the blessed privilege of communing with thee . . ."3

I share much with that woman lying awake in the tent, and yet we are far apart in time and distance and perspective.

And so, what began as a journey looking for traces of women's presence along the Oregon Trail has also become a journey of listening. Listening for the women's voices as they somehow blend with my own.

Come. . . . Look . . . and listen . . . with me.

CHAPTER ONE

The Oregon Trail
In Place And Time

**I am thinking while I write, Oh Oregon
you must be a lovely country**
—Amelia Stewart Knight, 1853

The National Frontier Trails Center is in a low-key corner of Independence, a few blocks away from Harry Truman's place. Here, you can take an intriguing journey. Three, in fact. A huge map on the wall in front of you shows the three westward trails that took off from Independence and changed our history.

Above the map are the words of an Oregon Trail traveler:

> **It is remarkable how anxious these
> people are to hear from the Pacific
> country and strange that so many . . .
> should sell out comfortable homes . . .
> pack up and start across such an
> immense, barren waste to settle in
> some new place of which they have at
> most so uncertain information, but this
> is the character of my countrymen.**
> —James Clyman, 1846

From the map, you can choose from among the three paths through the Center that trace the major trails west. Poignant diary excerpts, photographs, and paintings tell the travelers' stories.

One path takes you on the Santa Fe Trail, which opened up in 1822. It was first a men-only trading trail, then a military trail in the war with Mexico. Take another turn and you can follow the path from Independence along the Blue Rivers to the great Platte River Road, where Mormons, beginning in 1846, followed the north side to their promised land. Non-Mormons bound for Oregon or California followed the south side, at least in the beginning.

Trace the Platte, with its tales of dust and mud and boredom and storms and death from cholera across what is now Nebraska and into Wyoming, where you follow the Sweetwater River to a place known as the Parting of the Ways. This was just one of the places where wagon trains divided. Here sisters, brothers, parents, friends, enemies, lovers separated, bound for separate lives. Some would meet again. Most would not.

Here, you decide if you're going to follow the journey to California or to Oregon Country. The dangerous southwestern trail took the travelers to the fertile farmlands, gold and adventure of California. The equally-dangerous northwest route led to Oregon, the "garden of Eden," where "the clover grows wild, . . . and when you wade through it, it reaches your chin." Or so the weary travelers were told.

As more people trekked west, the trails became travel corridors, with arteries branching out every whichway. The corridors generally followed the river routes traveled by American Indians and trappers. Today, the major highway systems follow those early travel corridors.

At the National Frontier Trails Center, you learn an important distinction. While the people were traveling to their destination to settle, they were emigrants (or immigrants, depending on whether they thought of themselves as going or coming). Once they settled, they were pioneers. That's why you hardly ever see the word "pioneer" as you travel the Oregon Trail.

The Oregon Trail became known as the family trail. Single men without the encumbrances of family were more likely to head for California, which became known as the path of the renegades and adventurers. Oregonians themselves became downright snooty about this distinction. To this day in Oregon, the story goes that at a branch on the trail, a pile of gold quartz marked the way to California, while a sign lettered "To Oregon" directed the travelers north. Those who could read turned north.[1]

Between 250,000 to 500,000 people traveled west on the Oregon and California Trails from 1843 to 1860, and more than half headed for California. Ninety percent of those who started out made it. No one knows how many of those who failed to reach their destination turned back or died on the trail, but the number of trail deaths reached into the tens of thousands.

Oregon's Anglo population by 1860 was 52,000, with an estimated three men to every two women. A relatively small number of Oregon Trail emigrants were black—some slaves, some free. Free Blacks headed for California or Washington Territory because of the 1844 Oregon Exclusion Act, which barred free Blacks from acquiring land.

Our guide at the National Frontier Trails Center is Bill Bullard, the Center administrator. With his white beard and lean build, he looks like he'd be perfectly at home bullwhacking across the prairies himself. As he takes us along the Oregon Trail path, he fills us in on more of its background.

First, the Oregon Trail wasn't a trail at all in most places on the prairie. "There were all kinds of trails," Bullard tells us. "The emigrants would spread out across the prairie, sometimes scattered four or five miles, to get out of each other's dust. And they'd only come together at night or at river or narrow hill or mountain crossings." That's why you're not likely to see trail ruts when you're traveling in prairie country.

According to Bullard, men's fashions had a hand in the westward movement. Nineteenth-century men in the East liked beaver hats, and beavers were in the West. The fur traders—the notorious

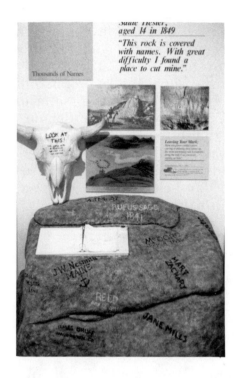

National Frontier
Trails Center
Independence, MO

mountain men—were among the first white men to push into western lands. First came the French-Canadians, then the Americans and the British.

Lewis and Clark and their Corps of Discovery's 1804 expedition took them across the northern part of the Rockies through what is now Wyoming, Montana, and Idaho to the Columbia River and finally the Pacific Ocean. The Lewis and Clark expedition didn't open up a western migration route for families, but the explorers laid the groundwork for American claim in Oregon Territory.

During the 1830s, missionaries began going west, bringing the Gospel to the "heathen Indians" as part of the evangelical fervor sweeping the country. Both the trappers and the missionaries returned to "the States" with wondrous tales of rich western lands.

By the 1840s, spurred by the terrible depression of 1837, emigration fever took hold, and the first wagon trains began to head west. Those early travelers were going on a hope and a promise of free land, because the US didn't yet have claim to those lands. Oregon Country—by a "gentlemen's agreement"—was held jointly by the US and Great Britain. The thinking was that the more US settlers that occupied the lands, the greater the chances those lands would one day belong to the US. And that's pretty much how it happened.

Paden Collection

Bullard brings to our attention a corner display. It's the Paden collection, artifacts collected by Irene D. Paden, who traveled the trails during the 1930s and wrote the classic *The Wake of the Prairie Schooner*. Here, you see tools and utensils the emigrants began their journey with and had to discard along the way, to be picked up by Paden nearly a century later. There's an iron cooking pot, a candle holder, a flour scoop, a flatiron. Gazing at these things once used by women valiantly trying to hold fragile lives and families together, the imagination takes off.

After she threw it away, what did the owner of the cooking pot prepare the food in? Was there food to cook? To think there wasn't even room to stash the candle holder. How did the woman light the night to tend a birth or a sick child? There are accounts of women actually ironing table cloths on the trail. By the time some woman discarded that iron, wrinkle-free aprons and tablecloths surely were no longer considered a necessity.

There's a wheel. A spur. And something I'd never seen: heavy iron discs used as snow shoes for horses and oxen. If animals needed snow shoes in winter weather, what protection did the emigrants have for their feet by the time they reached the lands of snow?

I remembered reading about Elizabeth Dixon Smith, who traveled from Indiana to Oregon in 1847 with her husband and their seven children. Traveling over mountains in November, she wrote:

> . . . it rains and snows . . . my
> children give out with cold and fatigue
> and could not travle and the boys had
> to unhitch the oxon and bring them and
> carry the children on to camp I was so
> cold and numb that I could not tell by
> feeling that I had any feet at all . . .

Two days later, she wrote:

> . . . rain all day it is all most an
> imposibility to cook and quite so to
> keep warm or dry I froze or chilled my
> feet so that I cannot wear a shoe so I
> have to go round in the cold water
> bearfooted.

Later, I would search Paden's book for descriptions of where she found the discarded treasures— maybe some stories behind them—but strangely, she wrote little about them.

She did write that by the time they'd traveled the length of the Platte, "the travelers had lost much of their cocksureness . . . . They were tired and (in cholera years) badly frightened. Their sense of values had changed. Things that had been great treasures when they were carefully packed for transportation to the new land, were now only extra weight wearing out the suddenly precious draught animals."

Bill Bullard points out words on the walls expressing the anguish of abandoning loved ones and belongings:

> **Father . . . died at the second**
> **crossing of Ham's Fork. We had two**
> **wagons, so mother had the men take**
> **the wagon bed of one of them to make a**
> **coffin. She abandoned the running gear,**
> **ox yokes, and some of our outfit, and**
> **we finished the trip with one wagon.**
> **—Elvina Apperson Fellows,**
> **age ten in 1847**

> **[A]t a meeting of the men of the**
> **wagon train it was decided to throw**
> **away every bit of surplus weight so that**
> **better speed could be made. . . . A man**
> **named Smith had a wooden rolling pin**
> **that it was decided was useless and**
> **must be abandoned.**

I shall never forget how that big man stood there with tears streaming down his face as he said, 'Do I have to throw this away? It was my mother's. I remember she always used it to roll out her biscuits, and they were awful good biscuits.'
    —Lucy Ann Henderson Deady,
                    age eleven in 1846

Bullard pauses before a startling photograph of a Plains Indian *standing* on a horse in tall grass. "The grass on the tall grass prairies between here and the Platte River grew so high that sometimes standing on a horse was the only way you could see what was ahead," he says. "You couldn't see a man on horseback. And you often couldn't see the wagon bottoms, so they really did look like 'prairie schooners' when all you could see was their 'sails.'

"The native grass had a massive, tough root system. Plows at the time couldn't cut through it. The Weston plow, which wasn't invented until the late 1850s, curved and cut under the roots. It was the Weston plow that allowed cultivation and settlement of the tall grass prairies."

Between the Missouri River and the West Coast lay the vast stretch of country they called the Great American Desert, Bullard explains. The grass prairies were impossible to plow, and beyond that were the sage prairies and treacherous mountains. The whole stretch was a land of extremes—cold winters, hot summers, poor soil, scarce water, and no trees. The Great American Desert, they believed, was uninhabitable. Uninhabitable, that is, by anyone but the Indians who, they had to believe, were "uncivilized."

In fact, according to Bullard, as early as the 1820s, the US government planned to "give" the Great American Desert to the American Indians. Already it was setting up a patchwork of reservations there for Indians forced off their own lands to the east as the Anglo invaders marched ever westward.

Ruth and I are running out of time, so we turn our attention to the rest of the words and photos and paintings telling the trail stories.

"Everyone who writes about the trails disagrees with everyone else," Bullard says philosophically. "So we just quote those who were there. Then there's no argument."

In their own simple and profound way, those who were there told of their journey in such a way that nothing need be added, no argument is necessary. There at the Center, diary excerpts narrate the journey, labeled by symbol according to whether the writer is a man, woman, girl child or boy child.

We read of encounters with Indians:

> **They looked so naked and wild. The men got out their guns, but all the Indians wanted was to see us and to see if we would give them anything.**
> —Lucy Ann Henderson Deady,
> age eleven in 1846

Buffalo along the Platte River:

> **Wood is now very scarce, but 'buffalo chips' are excellent—they kindle quick and retain heat surprisingly. We had this evening buffalo steaks broiled upon**

them that had the same flavor they
would have had on hickory coals.
—Tamsen Donner, 1846

Prairie storms:

I remember we were camped on the
Platte, the whole sky became black as
ink. . . . The rain came down in
bucketfuls, drenching us to the skin.
There wasn't a tent in the camp that
held against the terrific wind. The men
had to chain the wagons together to
keep them from being blown into the
river. . . . Finally, in spite of efforts of
the men, the cattle stampeded.
—Mary Elizabeth Munkers Estes,
age ten in 1846

River crossings:

A number of accidents happened
here. A lady and four children were
drowned through the carelessness of
those in charge of the ferry.
—Sallie Hester, 1849

Death on the trail:

Sixty miles from Fort Laramie . . .
Dear parents . . . John still continued
sick some times better and then worse
until the 7th of 6th month . . . I had to
bid him farewell and see him breathe
the last breath of earthly life without a
struggle or groan . . . The place where
we left him was nine miles from where
we had come to the Platte River close to
the roadside by a small grove.
—Rachel Fisher Mills, 1847

Life on the trail:

> Circles of white-tented wagons may
> now be seen in every direction, and the
> smoke from the campfires is curling
> upwards, morning, noon, and evening.
> An immense number of oxen and
> horses are scattered over the entire
> vally, grazing upon the green grass.
> Parties of Indians, hunters, and
> emigrants are galloping to and fro, and
> the scene is one of almost holiday
> liveliness. It is difficult to realize that
> we are in a wilderness, a thousand
> miles from civilization.
>
> —Edwin Bryant, 1846

A child's wondering:

> I remember one afternoon, . . . I got
> to wondering where we were trying to
> get to and asked the question, when
> someone said, 'To Oregon.'
> I did not know any more, but was
> satisfied, I think I made up my mind
> then and there not to ask that question
> any more.   .   . To me, 'Oregon' was a
> word without meaning.
>
> —Jesse A. Applegate, age seven in 1843

Dust:

> Very dusty roads. You in the States
> know nothing about dust. It will fly so
> that you can hardly see the horns of
> your tongue yoke. It often seems that
> the cattle must die for the want of
> breath, and then in our wagons such a
> spectacle, beds, cloths, victuals, and
> children, all completely covered.
>
> —Elizabeth Smith Geer, 1847

Mountain crossings:

> **In passing across these mountains,
> we were overtaken by a snow storm,
> which made the prospect very dismal. I
> remember wading through mud and
> snow and suffering from the cold and
> wet.**
> —Jesse A. Applegate, age seven in 1843

Dangerous cutoffs:

> **If we had kept the old road down the
> Columbia River—but three or four
> trains of emigrants were decoyed off by
> a rascally fellow who came out from
> the settlement in Oregon assuring us
> that he had found a near cut-off . . .
> The idea of shortening the long journey
> caused us to yield to his advice. Our
> sufferings from that time no tongue can
> tell.**
> —Tabitha Brown, 1846

The end of the trail:

> **We came . . . over the Cascades by
> the newly opened Barlow route, and it
> was a fierce route. The oldest child . . .
> had died before we started, and father
> died on the way across the plains, so
> when we reached Portland our family
> consisted of my mother and nine
> children . . .**
> **Mother had no money and had nine
> hungry mouths to feed in addition to
> her own, so she would go to the ships
> that came and get washing to do.**
> —Elvina Apperson Fellows,
> age ten in 1847

National Frontier
Trails Center
Independence, MO

The words and pictures on the walls tell thousands of stories, but something else catches our attention.

In the courtyard of the Trails Center stands an appealing, sturdy statue. A nameless, bonneted young woman gazes westward into the unknown. One arm cuddles and protects her baby. The other hand holds a bucket. She wears a long, plain dress over booted feet. Her apron billows with the wind.

I study the face of the young mother bravely facing whatever is to come. I think back to what Jane VanBoskirk, my actress friend, told me she learned from portraying emigrant and pioneer women. "Persist," they taught her. "Persist. When you have no other choice, you just keep going."

Yes. That's what I see on this woman's face. Persistence.

As I gaze at her, I wonder. Who is she? Where does she come from? What are her dreams? What does she see as she fixes her gaze westward?

CHAPTER TWO

Who Were These Women?

Mending, making, thus repairing
Woman's work is never done
—from "Woman's Work is Never Done"
Eighteenth-century English song

For most of the women who made the westward journey in the 1840s and early '50s, home was a farm in a Midwestern state—Indiana, Illinois, Iowa, Ohio, Kentucky, Tennessee, Missouri. They were family people. Rural people. Farm people. They were neither rich nor poor. The rich had no need to go and the poor couldn't raise the money. Most were on-the-edge middle class, many held property, and most had moved westward at least once before, like their parents and grandparents before them. Most would move again.

The mid-nineteenth century Midwestern farm economy was in transition from self-sufficiency to a cash-based economy. The farm family produced most of their needs, and bartered or bought the rest with proceeds from the farm surplus—much of it women's "cheese and eggs" money. Women were central to the family and the economy, and they kept careful track of money. Their lives consisted mainly of daily and seasonal routines of work—enough work to choke a horse, as my grandfather would have said.

> **In March it is mud, it is slush in**
> **December**
> **The midsummer breezes are loaded**
> **with dust**
> **In the fall the leaves litter, in muddy**
> **September**
> **The wallpaper rots and the candlesticks**
> **rust.**
> —"Housewife's Lament" (traditional)

These words are from a longer poem by an Illinois housewife named Sara A. Price in the 1850s. She is said to have borne seven children and lost them all, some to the Civil War. Her poem was found in her diary and later set to music as "The Housewife's Lament." Mrs. Price's poem graphically described the endless, gritty conditions farm women faced.

Was it mostly sweeping and dusting and potting and panning? For Midwestern farm women, that wasn't the half of it.

Folklorist Alan Lomax quoted one woman who spoke from experience:

> **You had to be a stout body to be a**
> **woman way up west in the Ohio**
> **wilderness. There wasn't no time to get**
> **outside the clearin'. Squash, pumpkins,**
> **potatoes, beans, beets, turnips and the**
> **rest of the garden truck to be planted,**
> **hoed and gathered. Made our own**
> **candles and spun our own flax and**
> **wool. The man of the house would go**
> **off hunting and git a deer or two, and**
> **then laze around between crops. But we**
> **never got away from the spinning**
> **wheel, the cooking fire and the baby's**
> **cradle. I remember a neighbor lady who**
> **picked up her knitting and knitted a**

**few rounds at her own husband's
funeral, she was so used to keeping
busy the whole time.**[1]

Punctuating his point, Lomax quoted a Midwestern tombstone:

**Thirteen years I was a virgin,
Two years I was a wife,
One year I was a mother,
The next year took my life.**

Keturah Penton Belknap was a Midwestern farm
woman who traveled on the Oregon Trail, and one
of the few who left a record of her life before the
journey. In journals and reminiscences, she recalled
her life in Ohio and Iowa from early childhood. Her
parents had moved three times, ever westward, from
New Jersey to Ohio. Their parents before them had
come from Sweden, Holland, Ireland, and England.

Beneath the matter-of-fact reporting emerges a
feisty, active young girl. I picture Kit, the ten-year-
old child, in perpetual motion, pigtails flying as she
chases after her four sisters and two brothers.

Besides helping her mother with "women's work,"
Kit (as her family called her) helped her father log
their land and once killed a deer with an axe. She
attended school sporadically, and often made the
six-mile trip into town on horseback through
"swales knee deep in mud and water" to get mail,
shop, and sell butter and cheese.

The teenaged Kit "was trying to support myself
and help the family some." Wages were low, and
she recorded once working for a whole week doing
house work and washing in exchange for one day
of a man's work to help her father harvest the
wheat crop.

A mother sits at the end of the day, contemplating the future of a daughter who has been help, friend and companion.

"I noticed Mother lingered over her tea and I thought she looked a little sad," Kit wrote. "Like she wanted to say something that was hard to say . . . ." The mother advised her daughter to get married and make her own home, lest she be "an old broken down old Maid and maybe so cross nobody would want [her] and then would be kicked about from one place to another without any home."

The options must have run through Kit's mind. When a whole week of her work was valued as a day of a man's work, how could she realistically make a living for herself? If she stayed home with her parents and became a "broken down old maid" . . . well, that was a terrible fate to ponder.

If a woman got to be twenty-five and wasn't married, that's what she was—an old maid or a spinster. ("Spinster," by the way, means a woman who spins all day.) The other women would gossip about her:

> **No one in his sense would marry an old maid of twenty-five or past. . . . Why, they made butter with cow tracks in it, it was so vile smelling. . . . They were the kind of people who . . . let the fire go out, who had to borrow soft soap, who didn't keep the weevils out of their seed peas, who let their gourds get soggy.[2]**

Still, being single did have its advantages . . .

> **Single girl, single girl,**
> **goin' where she please,**
> **A married girl, a married girl,**
> **has a baby on her knees.**
> **A single girl, single girl,**
> **wears clothes so fine,**
> **A married girl, a married girl,**
> **wears just any old kind.**
> —"Single Girl" (traditional)

"So I told her then," Kit wrote, "when the right one came along Ide think the matter over and let her know . . . ."

Kit checked out some possibilities ("for their was about five single men to evry girl") and settled on George Belknap, whom she married in 1839. Kit was nineteen years old.

> **I love my mamma, and my papa, too,**
> **But I'd leave them both to go with you.**
> —"Careless Love" (traditional)

Two weeks later the newlyweds loaded a two-horse wagon and traveled four weeks to a make a new home in Iowa.

> **It seems real nice to have the whole**
> **control of my house; can say I am**
> **monarch of all I survey and there is**
> **none to dispute my right.**

> **The years have been much the same.**
> **This has been the most tedious winter I**
> **ever experienced.**

Keturah Belknap had been married three and a half years when she expressed these seemingly-contradictory sentiments within months of each other. We see her world narrowing from the wider world she knew as a child to her household domain. Although she was "monarch" of her home, the constant battles with relentless hard work and weather extremes—"April 1 and everything frozen solid yet"—must have worn her down.

When Kit set out on the Oregon Trail to become a pioneer, the fact is that she already had *been* a pioneer. After living with George's parents in a log cabin, the couple built a frame house on a quarter section (160 acres) of raw land the government had "bought of the Indians." On their farm, the couple raised corn, wheat, sheep, chickens, cows, and hogs. In the first eight years of her marriage, Kit bore four children.

Menu for Christmas Dinner, 1841
[Adapted from Kit's description]

For company, will have Father Belknaps [George's parents] and the Hawley family and most likely the preacher—12 in all.

Firstly; for bread, nice light rolls, cake, doughnuts.
For pie, pumpkin.
Preserves, crab apples and wild plums.
Sauce, dried apples.
Meat first round: roast spare ribs with sausage and mashed potatoes and plain gravy.

**Second round: chicken stewed with the
best of gravy; chicken stuffed and
roasted in the dutch oven by the fire.**

"Everything went off in good style," she reported, noting that she impressed the in-laws. "Some one heard the old folks say they had no idea Kit could do so well."

**Preserves
[adapted from
Kit Belknap's description]**

**Now I want to tell you how I make a
substitute for fruit. Take a nice large
water melon. Cut them in two and
scrape the inside fine to the hard rind
and it will be mostly water. When you
get a lot prepared strain it thru a seive
or thin cloth, squeeze out all juice you
can, then boil the juice down to syrup.
Take some good melons and crab apple,
about half and half, and put them in the
syrup and cook them down till they are
done, being careful not to mash them.
Put in a little sugar to take the flat off
and cook it down a little more and you
have nice preserves to last all winter.
(And they are fine when you have
nothing better and sugar is 12 1/2 cents
a lb. and go 40 miles after it.)**

The preferred nineteenth-century term for recipes was "receipts." An 1857 issue of *Godey's Lady's Book and Magazine* (the *Ladies Home Journal* of the nineteenth century) clarified the correct usage:

**A constant reader . . . takes us to
task for using 'Receipts' for 'Recipes.'**

> **We respectfully inform him that we are correct. Did he ever hear of Mackenzie's Fine Thousand Recipes, Mrs. Hale's Recipes, or Mrs. Widdifield's Recipe-Books? No. They are Receipt-Books. Recipe is the Latin term for Receipt, and is used by physicians. We stick to the English. As he wished us to do so, we have explained.**

And that, dear reader, is why women on the Oregon Trail exchanged "receipts" rather than "recipes."

There was no "receipt" for butter, but every farm wife had her favorite method. The "clabber" (coagulated milk) must be just the right temperature or the butter would be puffy or "specky." Then the dasher—the thing that mashes the butter—must be stroked just so for thirty minutes.

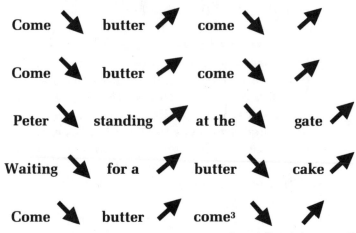

Come ↘ butter ↗ come ↘ ↗

Come ↘ butter ↗ come ↘ ↗

Peter ↘ standing ↗ at the ↘ gate ↗

Waiting ↘ for a ↗ butter ↘ cake ↗

Come ↘ butter ↗ come[3] ↘ ↗

(Arrows indicate dasher movement.)

If cooking was an endless job, so were spinning and sewing. John Mack Faragher, author of *Women and Men on the Overland Trail*, described the process of manufacturing cloth—homespun—from the raw materials of flax and wool. Flax (a fibrous plant) would be crushed and the fibers removed to be spun into yarn. After shearing, sheep wool would be washed, sorted according to its use, carded (combed), and spun. The women would weave the yarn on looms into wool and linen cloth or, more commonly, combine the yarns into linsey-woolsey (linen and wool).

Women wove the coarser tow cloth from the short fiber of the flax and used it for toweling, bandages, menstrual cloth, rags, some field clothing, and pillow and mattress ticking. The finest home-spun (linen) went into coverlets, tablecloths, and stitchery.

An old tradition held that before marriage, a girl would sew a linen (cambric) shirt for a young man as a promise to wed:

**You'll have for to make me a cambric
 shirt,
And every stitch must be finical work.**
 —"Strawberry Lane" (traditional)

For both women and men, underclothes "were not manufactured or worn," Faragher noted, "for they were considered an unnecessary extravagance."

Women commonly wore long slips, or chemises, under voluminous petticoats. On top, they would likely wear short corsets, loosely laced, in place of bras. Upper class ladies wore the notorious tightly-laced corsets to achieve wispy waists. These corsets were health hazards, causing shortness of breath, miscarriages and other problems. Only dress-up occasions might call for the farm woman to tighten up her laces.

Women would make their everyday clothes from homespun, and those who could afford it would sew their best clothes from "boughten" cloth. Kit Belknap wrote about sorting wool into short fiber for "comforts," the finest for flannels (for dresses), and the coarse wool for men's jeans.

Kit livened up the monotonous job of sorting wool by inviting "a dozen old ladies" in for a wool-picking party. Kit proudly served a "fine chicken dinner" and "old fashioned pound cake" like her mother had made. "[S]o now my name is out as a good cook so I am alright for good cooking makes good friends."

Working bees like the wool-picking parties nurtured friendships and knit together the community of women. Women's gatherings centered around work or church, for none could afford the luxury of simply being together without laboring for home, family or the Lord.

It was in the circle of friends that women shared news, gossip, advice on how to do their work, "receipts," remedies, and companionship. It was here where seeds of community were planted— seeds that grew into churches, schools, and support systems.

Quilting sustained and protected emigrant and pioneer women and their families—both the body and the soul. As one writer put it, "A woman made utility quilts as fast as she could so her family wouldn't freeze, and she made them as beautiful as she could so her heart wouldn't break."4

> I've been a hard worker all my life,
> but 'most all my work has been the
> kind that 'perishes with the usin', as the
> Bible says. That's the discouragin' thing
> about a woman's work . . . if a woman
> was to see all the dishes that she had to
> wash before she died, piled up before

**her in one pile, she'd lie down and die
right then and there. I've always had
the name o' bein' a good housekeeper,
but when I'm dead and gone there ain't
anybody goin' to think o' the floors I've
swept, and the tables I've scrubbed, and
the old clothes I've patched, and the
stockin's I've darned. . . . But when
one of my grandchildren or great-
grandchildren sees one o' these quilts,
they'll think about Aunt Jane, and,
wherever I am then, I'll know I ain't
forgotten.[5]**

—Aunt Jane of Kentucky

Women would make special quilts to mark life's
seasons of birth, coming of age, marriage and death.
Quilt patterns reflected the environments, the lives
and the creativity of their makers. The rich variety
of pattern names invokes a picture of pioneer life:
Mohawk Trail; Grandmother's Flower Garden; Log
Cabin; Little Red Schoolhouse; Pilgrim's Progress;
Job's Tears; Bear's Paw; Illinois Turkey Track;
Prairie Queen; Geese in Flight; True Lover's Knot;
Bride's Wreath; Barn Raising; Churn Dash; Pickle
Dish; Saw Tooth.

To prepare for a quilting bee, a woman first
designed and sewed the top layer, usually by
herself, or with help from family members. She
would then invite her friends to the bee, where
together they would sew the decorative top to an
anchoring bottom layer, with filler sandwiched
between. Sometimes they would invite the men to
join them afterwards for food, socializing and
perhaps a "play-party."

Play-parties were a way to get around religious prohibitions on dancing, and were usually for the younger crowd. At a play-party, the participants would play movement games to lively musical rhymes, which evolved into the square dancing we know today. Many of the play-party songs traveled on the trail: "Skip to my Lou," "Wait for the Wagon," "Pop Goes the Weasel," "Way Down Yonder in the Paw Paw Patch."

Quilting and social gatherings were welcome relief from jobs like the dreaded wash day. Universally, women hated wash day. Almost universally, they did it on Monday.

> **They that wash on Monday**
> **got all week to dry.**
> **They that wash on Tuesday**
> **are pretty near by**
> **They that wash Wednesday**
> **make a good house wife**
> **They that wash Thursday**
> **must wash for their life**
> **They that wash Friday must wash in need**
> **They that wash Saturday are sluts indeed.**[6]

The word "slut," by the way, had no sexual connotation here. It was a common epithet for a woman perceived to be lazy and slovenly. Any woman, that is, who was not busy working every waking hour. The proverb on washing doesn't mention Sunday. A woman who would wash on Sunday and break the Sabbath would be the worst kind of slut indeed.

Washing involved heating water in the washtub, pounding the clothes, wringing, rinsing, wringing again, and hanging them outside to dry. In sunshine or in below-zero weather. Faragher noted that the harsh lye soap and hot water chapped and cracked the skin, and the women's hands would often bleed into the tub.

Soap making was a complicated—even dangerous—job done two or three times a year. It involved pouring boiling water over wood ashes to form a caustic lye, adding scrap animal fats, and stirring the whole mess for long, hot hours, and this is the simplified version. "Soft soap" came first, and was hardened by adding salt during the boiling process and poured into molds. Soft soap could be used as a lubricant, especially for loose wooden bearings, and that's where the expression "soft soaping" comes from.

Meanwhile, back on the farm, the men worked hard too. They did the heavy, outdoor-oriented work: clearing forested land, constructing buildings and fences, plowing, planting, weeding, harvesting, repairing and maintaining tools. They herded, fed, tended, slaughtered and butchered the large animals, maintained barns and took products to market. As often as they could, they headed for the woods to go hunting or to town for business.

Women worked outside as well. They milked the cows, tended the chickens and marketed the dairy products. Where work overlapped, women would help the men plant and harvest, and often would cut fire wood. It would be a cold day in hell, though, before most men would admit to doing any "women's work."

As John Mack Faragher wrote, farm women "worked two or three hours more each day than the men, often spinning, weaving, or knitting late into the dark evening hours." Kit Belknap periodically mentioned her husband reading to her as she spun and sewed, extending her work day into the evenings.

Women's work on the farm was essential and expected, and rarely appreciated. One new husband interviewed on an Illinois river boat assessed the value of women's work this way:

> **I calculate 'taint of much account to have a woman if she ain't of no use . . . every man ought to have a woman to do his cookin' and such like, [because] it's easier for them than it is for us. They take to it kind o' naturally . . . I reckon women are some like horses and oxen, the biggest can do the most work, and that's what I want one for.[7]**

Mud and dirt compounded women's work on the farm. Faragher noted that "[t]he yard between the kitchen and barn was always covered with enough dung to attract hordes of summer houseflies. . . . In wet months the yard was a mess of mud, dung, and cast-off water, constantly tracked into the house."

> **There are worms on the cherries and slugs on the roses**
> **And ants in the sugar and mice in the pies**
> **The rubbish of spiders no mortal supposes**
> **And ravaging roaches and damaging flies.**
> **With grease and with grime from corner to corner**

Forever at war and forever alert
No rest for a day lest the enemy enter
I spend my whole life in a struggle with
dirt.

—"Housewife's Lament"

Flies. Dirt. They were the enemies, not only because they messed things up, but because they were deadly. Bacteria and viruses lurked in cities and farms alike, to spread diseases through flies and dirt and dung. An 1843 traveler in the Mississippi Valley found malaria (swamp fever) everywhere: "I can hear of no spot high or low . . . that is not invaded. To find a single family some member of which has not had a chill or two would be a curiosity."[8] Death rates were high, and at least one of every five children died before reaching their fifth birthday.

Typhoid (valley fever), cholera, scarlet fever and tuberculosis stalked the land, aggravated by poor sanitary practices such as common drinking cups, towels and wash basins. Asiatic cholera periodically swept westward from European trade routes. Ironically, those hoping to escape the terrible disease would take it with them along the trail.

In rural areas, women were the healers before medicine became a licensed practice barring women. Women would cultivate their handed-down lore and their herb garden remedies for comfort, if not always healing.

Three little angels
Come from the North
Take away fire
Put in frost.

Say this while rubbing a burn gently
nine times. (This will only work if told
by a man to a woman or a woman to a
man.)[9]

Some of their wisdom they learned from American Indian lore, but they couldn't keep up with the diseases that periodically ravaged the countryside and stole their loved ones.

Kit Belknap tries to comfort her child struggling for breath. Some time after it is over, she takes her pen and writes. It is November 1843.

I have experienced the first real trial of my life. After a few days of suffering our little Hannah died of lung fever so we are left with one baby.

Another year passes. Another child dies. Another is born.

By now Kit dares not hope her children will grow up. "It has never been well so we have two children for a while; neither of them are very strong."

Of the four children born to Kit and George Belknap on their Iowa farm, three died in infancy. One child was left to accompany his parents on the trail.

Abide with me, fast falls the eventide
The darkness deepens, Lord with me
**   abide!**
When other helpers fail, and comforts
**   flee,**
Help of the helpless, O abide with me.
                    —Traditional Methodist hymn

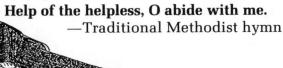

Religion offered a source of comfort and connection for women in the mid-nineteenth-century Midwest. The solace of believing that hard work and sacrifice and sorrow would find its reward in a life beyond this one must have kept many of them from just giving up.

Religion was a central part of Kit Belknap's life. She wrote of family trips to camp meetings, and of Methodist church meetings in her family's home when there was no church building. In her diary, she wrote, "As for me and my house we will serve the Lord."

Comforting as it was, religion was hardly a matter of choice for these women. Deemed intellectually inferior but morally superior to men, women were expected to uphold religious tradition within the family and community. One male authority declared that "female irreligion is the most revolting feature in human character."[10]

In the chaos of nineteenth-century changing society—religious awakening, economic fluctuations, westward migration, and, most importantly, the Industrial Revolution—something had to remain constant, and that was Womanhood. So the Cult of True Womanhood was born, as described by historian Barbara Welter in her classic 1966 essay, "The Cult of True Womanhood."

The True Woman was to be all that man was not: pious, pure, submissive, and domestic. She was to be religious, protective of her sexual purity, submissive to her wiser husband, and guardian of the home as haven for men. In its purest sense, the Cult of True Womanhood put the leisured, upperclass woman in a True Woman box. She became a model for others, stigmatizing working women, single women, slave women, and Indian women.

**That home is her appropriate and
appointed sphere of action there cannot**

**be a shadow of doubt; for the dictates
of nature are plain and imperative on
this subject, and the injunctions given
in Scripture no less explicit.**
—*Godey's Ladies Book* (July 1832)

While the Cult of True Womanhood defined who the True Woman was, the Cult of Domesticity defined her place. Farm women, who knew no leisure and had to muck around in the barnyards, couldn't aspire to the impossible ideal of True Womanhood, but they knew—and fiercely protected—their place as keepers of home and family.

"Women's status was through the family," says Lillian Schlissel, author of *Women's Diaries of the Westward Journey.* "That was their *only* status."

It's not surprising, then, that women took this Cult of Domesticity with them on the trail west. It explains the crisp, ironed, white aprons and table cloths. The fancy-as-possible meals. The determination to keep the Sabbath holy. The insistence on wash day, onerous chore though it may be. The resistance to wearing unladylike bloomer-type clothing, or riding astride a horse rather than side-saddle. An "unladylike" woman with a sunburn, calloused hands, horseback riding skills or independent opinions risked being labeled a slut or a scold. Until and unless, that is, unladylike behavior became a matter of survival.

Under the Cult of Domesticity, marriage was the only socially-accepted state for women, and for men as well. Marriages were rooted in pragmatism, rarely in romance or even mutual respect. Marriage was a practical matter, rarely a romantic choice. As Alan Lomax wrote, "Love was something you laughed at or died of."

The Cult of Domesticity tied women to home, while the Cult of Individualism propelled their men ever outward and westward. Men and women came to define themselves and each other less by who they were than by who they were not. Men were not-women. Women were not-men.

The separation of the sexes resulted in two cultures. Men's culture was one of rugged individualism, one-upmanship and male camaraderie. Women's culture was one of home and family and a community of women exchanging lore and advice and support. Not surprisingly, sparks flew when the Cult of Domesticity and the Cult of Individualism crashed together.

Legal and cultural practices enforced the separation of the sexes, keeping both women and men in their places. Any money the wife earned, any property she inherited, any children the couple had—all legally belonged to the husband, who also had the legal right to determine where the family would live.

If a woman didn't work hard enough or if she were uppity or complaining, she was subject to verbal or even physical abuse. Although American law protected women on paper from domestic violence, women could not sue, so they could not turn to the courts for protection. Divorce was difficult and socially abhorrent. We don't know the extent of domestic violence in the nineteenth century, but it was at least tacitly sanctioned— inherited from religion, British law, and tradition.

> **A woman, a dog, a hickory tree,**
> **The more you beat them the better they**
> **be.**
>
> —old English saying,
> popular in the Midwest

The "rule-of-thumb" comes from British law that approved a man beating an unruly wife with a stick, as long as the stick wasn't any thicker than a man's thumb.

Calvinist preachers reminded women that they were created to nurture and be pious and pure. But, they warned, as descendents of Eve, women brought evil to mankind, and if they wavered from their God-ordained domestic and dependent roles, they risked reverting to their evil origins.

Midwestern popular songs and lore reinforced the "devil's-in-woman" theme. Witch stories, nearly as common as ghost stories, warned of evil women in league with the devil who could stop cream from turning into butter, or turn a man into a horse, or herself into a cat.

And now you see
what a woman can do,
She can outdo the devil
and her old man too.
—"The Farmer's Curst Wife" (traditional)

Murder ballads, imported from the British Isles, described grisly deaths of fair young lasses who overstepped their bounds—ballads that, according to Alan Lomax, "provided fantasy revenge upon the whole unsatisfactory, demanding feminine sex."

He took the brown girl by the hand
And led her in the hall
And there with a sword cut off her
head
And dashed it against the wall.
—"Lord Thomas and Fair Elinore"
(traditional)

Women got their revenge in song:

> **Then he turned his back around**
> **And faced yon willow tree,**
> **She caught him around the middle so**
> **small**
> **And throwed him into the sea.**
> —"Lady Isabel and the Elf Knight"
> (traditional)

The ideal woman was either gone or dead, never alive and working beside you.

> **I dream of Jeannie**
> **with the light brown hair . . .**
> —popular song by Stephen Foster

> **But the only object on my mind**
> **was the girl I left behind.**
> —"The Girl I left Behind" (traditional)

Songs even remotely complimentary of wives were unheard of:

> **I married a wife, o then, o then,**
> **I married a wife, o then,**
> **I married a wife, she's the curse of my**
> **life**
> **And I wish I was single again.**
> —"When I Was Single" (traditional)

Women weren't inclined to compliment men either:

> **I know we are much nicer**
> **Than ugly horrid men,**
> **We do not chew tobacco,**
> **We do not cuss like them;**

We do not drink cheap whiskey,
We don't get on a bust,
The boys don't have to watch us,
For girls will do to trust.[11]
—"The Boys Won't Do To Trust"
(traditional)

The stage was set for separate journeys side by side along the trail leading westward. Women trying to hold some semblance of home and community together. Men moving forward no matter the cost, trying to maintain a facade of toughness even when they felt vulnerable and frightened.

"My intuition is that women and men had opposite visions on the trail," says Lillian Schlissel. "Men wanted land. Women wanted to hold their families together. It's generally clear among historians that women did not make the decision to go. They were reluctant travelers for the most part. They were backward looking, leaving part of themselves behind. Yet they were realistic enough to know that they could improve their condition."

The woman in stone in the courtyard facing westward. Perhaps she sees a better future.

But oh the price.

CHAPTER THREE

Oregon Fever!

**He had a notion to go west,
   he was the restless sort
And Lord knows, land was scarce,
   and our money always short
Still I cried the day he told me,
   and I begged for us to stay
He only said we're goin'—
   it's best we don't delay**
              —"Overland 1852"

They called it Oregon Fever. Maybe it was a fever. It kind of snuck up on you and grabbed you and held on. At least that's how it was for the men.

Causes of this fever were many. Mainly it was money and land—either not having enough, or fearing you could lose what you have, or wanting more. The 1837 depression that swept the country brought on bank closures, low wages and glutted markets. In the Midwest, grain brought such low prices that steamboats on the Mississippi and Missouri Rivers were burning the crops for fuel. By the 1840s, the depression had eased, but people were jumpy.

Oregon Fever had other causes too. Men watched their children, and sometimes their wives, die of "fever, ague, consumption" and the other maladies that kept whole communities of people gaunt and pale and fearful.

Surely there was some place better than this— some place where a man could have acres of land paid for with his own sweat and perseverance.

Some place where you could live with your family on your own farm and make a good living for yourself. Some place where you wouldn't see your neighbor's smoke. A place where you and your wife and children wouldn't feel poorly. A place where a man wouldn't freeze in the winter and labor under the scorching sun in the summer, and wonder if the weather would play tricks on your crops and turn them to dust.

> **Come along, come along—don't**
> **be alarmed,**
> **Uncle Sam is rich enough**
> **to give us all a farm.**[1]
> > —popular camp song

There was such a place. That's what the guidebooks to Oregon said, and the missionaries too—the ones who went west to save souls and instead discovered a wondrous land, just waiting to be cleared, plowed and planted. When you've got a chance to start over in a land of promise, you've got to grab it before it's gone.

Besides, wasn't it America's destiny to keep moving west so that one day this great country would reach from sea to shining sea?

And then there was the adventure of it. This quest would require all the courage and skills a man could muster, to take family and wagons and animals and supplies across 2,000 ominous miles, facing dangerous animals and the elements and the Indians, to get to this place called Oregon.

Yes, there was Some Place Else. Besides, you had moved Some Place Else before so you knew how to do it. You thought maybe you had settled down then, but . . .

> **I think I'll settle down,**
> **and I says, says I,**

I'll never wander further
till the day I die.
But the wind it sorta chuckles—
Why of course you will,
For once you git the habit,
you just can't keep still . . .[2]
   —Nineteenth century ditty

This restlessness was indeed a habit. The longing for Some Place Else grabbed the men again, and pulled them clear across half a continent toward the unsettled and unknown land in the fabled place of Oregon.

Women recognized the symptoms of Oregon Fever. They'd seen these symptoms of hankering for Some Place Else before.

> **This past winter there has been a**
> **strange fever raging here (it is the**
> **Oregon fever) it seems to be contagious**
> **and it is raging terribly, nothing seems**
> **to stop it but to tear up and take a six**
> **months trip across the plains with ox**
> **teams to the Pacific Ocean.**
>   —Kit Belknap, 1847

Kit Belknap sees the symptoms and all she can do about it is write in her diary.

> **Some of our friends have started for**
> **Oregon. . . . They will meet others at**
> **the crossing of the Missouri River and**
> **make laws and join together in a large**
> **company.**

Kit had not seen her parents since her marriage eight years before. It was time to make the journey back to Ohio to be with old friends and family. She worried about the health of her sickly child, as well as her own health "going into consumption."

> **I knew it would be the last visit I
> would make there whether I lived or
> not but I kept all these thots buried in
> my own breast and never told them
> that the folks at home were fixing to
> cross the plains while we were away
> but taking it all around we had a good
> time. We were there a month, then it
> came time to say good bye. The last few
> days the baby was growing weaker and
> I wanted to get home where it could be
> more quiet. . . .**
>
> **It was hard for me to not break down
> but they all thot in about two years we
> would come again.**

Kit returned to Iowa to "all excitement about Oregon" and the news that her home had been sold and that her family was to live with her in-laws until they would leave for Oregon.

> **There was nothing done or talked of
> but what had Oregon in it and the loom
> was banging and the wheel buzzing and
> trades being made from daylight till bed
> time . . .**

Once again Kit Belknap watches helplessly and tries to comfort her child struggling for breath. Her sick child dies. She was one year and one month old. She takes her pen and writes. It is October 1847.

**Now we have one little baby boy left.
So now I will spend what little
strength I have left getting ready to
cross the Rockies.**

Two weeks after the death of her child—her own home sold, living in another family's home, and only one of her four children still alive—Kit is already making preparations for the journey.

**Have cut out four muslin shirts for
George and two suits for the little boy
(Jessie). With what he has that will last
him (if he lives) . . .**

Keturah Belknap left one of the most complete records in existence of preparation for the Oregon Trail journey. Her family was one of the minority that reached Oregon without losing a family member or suffering a major catastrophe. Kit's meticulous planning and day-and-night preparations were largely responsible for her family's safe passage.

But how would she know what to take? How much? How to pack it? She would have to rely on her own experience and intuition and advice from family and friends, because she couldn't rely entirely on the guidebooks.

Buffalo are in greatest abundance,
killed with the greatest facility.
—Lansford W. Hastings
The Emigrants' Guide to
Oregon and California

Overly-enthusiastic men wrote Oregon Trail guidebooks for men, predicting a relatively easy four-month trip in good health, if their directions were followed. Trouble was, some guidebook authors hadn't even been over the routes they recommended.

"Lansford Hastings was one of the great villains of the westward movement," declares Bill Bullard of the National Frontier Trails Center. "He wrote about routes of the trail without having been through it. He hadn't even been the whole route of what became known as the Hastings cutoff." That's where the Donner party, bound for California, got in trouble. Traveling late, they took a route Hastings had recommended but had not traveled. The fated wagon train, begun in high spirits, ended up trapped in a seasonal Sierra Nevada storm, and many died.

Hastings' guidebook and others neglected such topics as women's and children's clothing, cooking with buffalo chips, personal needs and medicines. What most guidebooks did advise women, according to Julie Roy Jeffrey, author of *Frontier Women*, was that women "must develop the male characteristics of strength and resilience, and resourcefulness to survive the trip and also to rely on their female qualities to soothe and socialize men, and to ensure social stability on the way west." That's pretty much what the women did.

It is October 1848. The family will leave with
their wagons for their "jumping-off place" of St.
Joseph on the Missouri River by April.

Kit Belknap sits down and tries to think through
how she will prepare for this journey across 2,000
miles of the unknown. She takes her pen and
writes.

> Now, I will begin to work and plan to
> make everything with an eye to starting
> out on a six month trip. The first thing
> is to lay plans and then work up to the
> program so the first thing is to make a
> piece of linen for a wagon cover and
> some sacks; will spin mostly evenings
> while my husband reads to me.

Sewing will be the biggest task: clothing for the
family, a double canvas cover for the wagon,
bedding, food sacks. She must make several pounds
of soap and stock cooking utensils, personal items
and medicine.

These are the physical preparations. But how
does she prepare her soul for such a thing? How
does she decide what treasures to pack? Which
books? Which remembrances of loved ones she
may never see again? Which quilts? Which linens?

And how will she wrench herself away from her
friends, her church, her community, knowing that
she likely will never see this place, these people
again?

In March she writes:

> I dont want to leave my kind friends
> here but they all think it best so I am
> anxious to get off. I have worked almost
> day and night this winter, have the
> sewing about all done but a coat and
> vest for George.

While the women spun, sewed, and stored up provisions, the men had their own considerable work to do. First came the job of raising the necessary cash for the journey, usually by selling the farm, equipment and household effects. Some borrowed the money or called in debts. Some left debts. In his reminiscences, A. H. Garrison remembered his father putting their farm up for sale in the fall for $1,500, and taking $800 for it in March, just before the family left.

Basic outfitting costs ran   close to $1,000 (equivalent to roughly $20,000 in today's dollars), including the wagon, draft animals, food, whiskey, firearms and gear. Whiskey? Strictly for medicinal and celebratory purposes, they would tell you. Add to these costs the money needed for ferries, equipment replacement, and food and shelter once the travelers reached their destination.

Smaller families would travel with just one wagon, while larger families took two or even three. The Belknap family traveled with five other families, each with one or two wagons and four yoke (eight) of oxen to a wagon.

The wagon had to be the right size—large enough to carry more than a ton of provisions, and small enough to make it through the rugged passageways along the trail. The large Conestoga wagons hauled loads on the freight trails, rarely families on the trails west. On my own journey, one park ranger explained it this way: "Picture the Conestoga as a semi-truck, and a prairie schooner as a U-Haul."

This emigrant version of "do-it-yourself-moving" should be waterproof so it would float at river crossings. The contents would be protected by two canvas cloths stretched over a frame. By the end of the trip, if there was anything left of the wagon, the canvas would be torn to shreds.

To pull that prairie schooner with perhaps 2500 pounds of weight required at least two yoke of oxen. The emigrants would need extra oxen to share the load, and to replace the animals that would almost surely die before reaching Oregon.

Horses and mules could haul the wagons too— and faster, but they were more expensive and more were needed for the job. And those cussed mules needed skilled, mean drivers. Mules lived up to their reputation for stubbornness, and mule teamsters weren't called muleskinners for their gentleness.

Our men are all well-armed. William carries a brace of pistols and a bowie knife. Aint that blood-curdling? I hope he won't hurt himself!
—Lucy Cooke, 1852

The men packed firearms for protection and for killing animals to supplement the food supply, although they would actually provide little of the food along the trail. They would be much more likely to kill or wound themselves or one another by accident than they were to be done in by Indians.

Now, picture putting everything you will need for six months on the road and setting up house-keeping at the road's end into a wooden box that measures four by ten feet.

Pack the wagon, woman, we are leaving Tennessee.
—"Overland 1852"

It's a delicate balance. Too little food and supplies and you risk starvation or freezing, or breaking down for lack of adequate equipment for repairs. Too much and you risk breaking down, wearing out the oxen or the wagon, or getting behind schedule and getting caught in winter storms.

According to Bill Bullard, besides taking bad advice, another mistake the Donner party made was having too fancy, too heavy wagons. They had fallen behind almost from the beginning of the trip and were late crossing the Rockies.

So how do you know how much to pack? The staple diet would be bread, bacon, and coffee. Lansford Hastings recommended for each emigrant 200 pounds of flour, 150 pounds of bacon, 10 pounds of coffee, 20 pounds of sugar and 10 pounds of salt. Women made linen sacks for these staples. Some goods would be packed in barrels that would hold water when empty of food. Add rice, chipped beef, dried beans, dried fruit, pickles, herbs and spices.

Kit Belknap described first packing a big box containing staples,

> . . . with a cover made of light boards
> nailed on two pieces of inch plank
> about 3 inches wide. This will serve us
> for a table, there is a hole in each
> corner and we have sticks sharpened at
> one end so they will stick in the
> ground; then we put the box cover on,
> slip the legs in the holes and we have a
> nice table, then when it is on the box
> George will sit on it and let his feet
> hang over and drive the team.

End of the Oregon Trail Museum
Oregon City, OR

Next, chests and boxes for clothes, medicine and
dishes. "[T]here will be cleats fastened to the
bottom of the wagon bed to keep things from
slipping out of place." And there's space for Kit's
rocking chair and for little Jessie to play.

Next, sacks of flour and corn meal.

Now comes the groceries. We will
make a wall of smaller sacks stood on
end; dried apples and peaches, beans,
rice, sugar and coffee, the latter being
in the green state. We will brown it in a
skillet as we want to use it. Everything
must be put in strong bags; no paper
wrappings for the trip. There is a
corner left for the wash-tub and the
lunch basket will just fit in the tub. The
dishes we want to use will all be in the
basket. I am going to start with good
earthen dishes and if they get broken
have tin ones to take their place. Have
made 4 nice little table cloths so am
going to live just like I was at home.

Preserved food would last them well into the trip.
Jane Maynard recorded the following receipts in
her journal before she began her 1867 journey to
settle in Idaho.

Pickle for Beef
(adapted with permission from the
diary of Jane Maynard, 1867)
First thoroughly rub salt into your
beef and let it remain in bulk 1 1/2
hours, then drain off the blood. Take it
. . . and let it drain, . . . and pack as
desired. Have ready a pickle prepared
as follows. For 100 lbs of beef use 7 lb
of salt petre, l lb of cayenne pepper, l qt
of molasses, 8 gallons soft-water, boil,
skim well. When cold pour over the
beef.

To preserve Eggs
(adapted with permission from the
diary of Jane Maynard, 1867)
For every three gallons of water put
in one pint of fresh stocked lime, one
half pint common salt. Mix well. Let the
barrel be about half full of this fluid.
With a dish let your eggs down, tipping
the dish so they will roll out so not to
crack the shell. If the shell cracks the
eggs spoil.

The emigrants found ingenious ways to pack their wagons. They sewed pockets in the canvas slides to tuck treasures in, kept eggs inside flour and corn meal, and bacon inside bran to keep the meat from turning rancid. Barrels could hold staples until the food ran out. The empty barrels would hold water later on as they trudged through the waterless western deserts. One woman described "long boxes like window gardens" along the sides of the wagon, containing sewing materials "and various odds and ends dear to the housewife's heart."

According to the authors of *Hearts and Hands: The Influence of Women and Quilts on American Society*, friendship quilts reached their height of popularity during the 1840s and 1850s—a time of great social mobility and the westward migrations.

Before a woman's departure on the trail, her friends would gather in a flurry of sewing and quilting bees to help her finish her tasks. Often the quilting bees would be "ceremonial leave-takings," according to *Hearts and Hands*. Friends would sew quilt blocks together with care and love, inscribing each with its maker's signature or message. Carried with them, the quilts would be a reminder of home and friends. Abandoned on the trail, it would be like leaving pieces of your heart along the way.

**And my friends, I thought my heart
would break to leave them all
behind . . .**
—"Overland 1852"

End of the Oregon
Trail Museum
Oregon City, OR

In the months before she left, Kit Belknap's friends came to help her sew. Their labor finished, it is time for Kit to leave. Time for friends to say "remember me."

**When far away from this dear spot
In a distant land do thou in
[Trust] pray, and when it is
[Well]with you, remember me.**[3]
—Lucy B. Lillie Webster Mays
inscription on a block from a
friendship quilt by
Betsey M. Wright Lee of Connecticut
pieced between 1846 and 1851.

**Leaving my dear mother who I never
more will see . . .**
—"Overland 1852"

Kit has already said good-bye to her mother and father and family back in Ohio. Now it is time to say good-bye to home and friends in Iowa.

> **We have had our farwell meeting so I wont go [to the regular Sunday meeting]; don't think I could stand it . . .**
> **Dr. Walker calls at the wagon to see me and give me some good advice and give me the parting hand for neither of us could speak the word 'Farewell.'**

She records no tears. Perhaps no tears are left.

Often, an entire community would come out for the leave-taking, and some neighbors might accompany the departing party for several miles, delaying the good-bye as long as possible.

Martha Gay Masterson was thirteen when her family left on the Oregon Trail journey from Springfield, Missouri in 1851. She remembered that on the day they left home,

> **Some friends had spent the night with us and others arrived at daylight. All places of business and the schools were closed during the forenoon, and everybody came to say good-bye to us. From early morning till ten o'clock they came. The house and yard and streets were crowded with people. Friends and schoolmates were crying all around us. . . . The sad farewells were all spoken.**

We took a long last look at all, then
closed our eyes on the scene and moved
forward. Their wails reached us as we
moved away.[4]

Farewell!

Who is there that does not recollect
their first night when started on a long
journey, the wellknown voices of our
friends still ring in our ears, the parting
kiss feels still warm upon our lips, and
that last separating word Farewell!
sinks deeply into the heart. It may be
the last we ever hear from some or all
of them, and to those who start . . .
there can be no more solemn scene of
parting only at death.[5]

—Lodisa Frizzell, 1852

CHAPTER FOUR

Who's Gonna Shoe Your Pretty Little Foot? Who'll Provide Your Table?

**Who's gonna shoe your pretty little
    foot?**
Who's gonna glove your hand?
> —traditional song

**The ladies have the hardest
    that emigrate by land,
For when they cook with buffalo wood
    they often burn a hand**[1]
> —"Crossing the Plains"
> by John A. Stone

The woman facing westward. How and where will she find and prepare enough food for herself and her family? The long skirt she wears. How does she expect to cross half a continent wearing skirts that sweep the dusty, muddy ground and get in the way?

As Ruth and I drive along the Kansas Interstate, we admire the peaceful grass-and-tree-filled landscape that zips by. We innocently comment on what a luxury a motel room—any room—would have been for the already travel-weary woman, worn from incessant cooking and dirt and the needs of husband and children.

We stop for an early dinner and start looking for a motel. Each little town we come to either has no motel or a NO VACANCY sign on the one it does have.

It's getting dark. I stop at a No Vacancy motel. They're not kidding. University of Kansas football fans have booked all the rooms for miles around. The sympathetic motel owner calls around and finds us a room twenty-five miles out of our way to the north.

We drive into the darkness of Kansas farm country that I swear could use more civilization— like motels. A half hour later there's no sign of a motel. No sign of a town or a farm or anything but dark.

"Are you sure we're on the right road?" Ruth asks.

Sure I'm sure. Until she asked. I wonder how many women on the trail wondered the same thing.

We arrive at the only motel in Onaga, Kansas. It's 10:00.

As I turn off my ignition and open the door, a man approaches my car and inspects the license plate.

"Geez, what're you doing here all the way from O-re-gone?"

"Long story," I mutter, impatient to start unpacking.

"Well, you look tired. I'll bet you could use a cold drink." He grins and offers two cans of beer.

I gratefully accept.

"Me and my buddies are huntin' quail so we brought plenty of beer," he says, nodding in the direction of a pickup. "Help yourself. There's more in the back of my truck over there."

We find our room, savor the beer and flop down onto our beds at the end of our day. Cold beer. Even the women would have appreciated cold beer on the trail.

Out there on the plains, the end of an exhausting, dirty day of travel brought the women long hours of work.

> **Although there is not much to cook, the difficulty and inconvenience in doing it, amounts to a great deal—so by the time one has squatted around the fire and cooked bread and bacon, and made several dozen trips to and from the wagon—washed the dishes (with no place to drain them) . . . and gotten things ready for an early breakfast, some of the others already have their night caps on.[2]**
>
> —Helen Carpenter, 1857

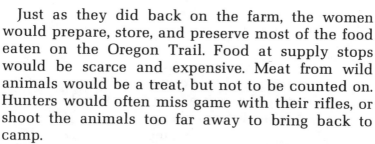

Just as they did back on the farm, the women would prepare, store, and preserve most of the food eaten on the Oregon Trail. Food at supply stops would be scarce and expensive. Meat from wild animals would be a treat, but not to be counted on. Hunters would often miss game with their rifles, or shoot the animals too far away to bring back to camp.

For some, chickens would provide fresh eggs, and "milch" cows might accompany emigrant parties clear to Oregon, giving milk daily. Kept in a churn in the wagon during the day's bumpy trek, extra cream would turn to butter by evening. Toward the end of the journey, many animals would have died or become too weak to provide any sustenance.

From Kit Belknap, we have a "receipt" for butter from her 1848 journal and reminiscences:

Butter on the Oregon Trail
(adapted from the diary of Kit Belknap)
Milk the cows at night and strain the
milk in little buckets. Cover them up
and set them on the ground under the
wagon. In the morning, take off the nice
thick cream and put it in the churn.
Save the strippings [the last milk drawn
from the cow] from . . . the morning
milking and put it in the churn also.
After riding all day you have a nice roll
of butter so long as you have plenty of
grass and water.

If ever there was a time a woman needed to call on all the skills and creativity she could muster, preparing food on the Oregon Trail would be that time.

Improvise. Learn. Scrounge. Remember. Make do. Stretch. Barter.

The standard traveling menu of bacon (sowbelly), bread, and coffee challenged the most creative cook.

[O]ne does like a change and about
the only change we have from bread
and bacon is to bacon and bread.
—Helen Carpenter, 1857

As long as supplies lasted, dried fruit, beans, rice and pickles would add variety and ward off scurvy. The women would roast green coffee beans in a pan and grind them in a coffee mill. Bacon was sometimes eaten raw if there was no time to cook it. Beans could be baked in a hole in the ground filled with coals. Bread would come in different forms: hard biscuits, "slam-johns" (pancakes), or fresh bread baked on the trail.

Trail Bread
(adapted from a description by
Kathryn Troxel and other sources)
Stir together liberal quantities of soda and warm water. Add enough flour and salt to make a firm dough and knead it. Use a large tin pan as a kneading trough. You can knead the dough while sitting on the wagon seat if you don't have to walk. Flatten the bread to about one inch and place it in a skillet or Dutch oven with an iron lid. By the time the meat is fried and the coffee made, the bread will be done.

Sometimes the bread will burn and the center will be raw. You can avoid this by setting the dough to rise at night, and in the morning, fry it in small cakes in a pan. Turn it often to keep it from burning.

If mosquitoes are thick, they can get into the dough and turn it black. There is nothing you can do about this.

Missionary Narcissa Whitman made

Fried Cakes
Take a little flour & water & make
some dough, roll it thin, cut it into
square blocks, then take some beef fat
& fry them. You need not put either salt
or pearl ash in your dough. (1836)

Women would work valiantly to supplement the basic bread, bacon and coffee. Imagine the pride of serving strawberry dumplings on a white (by then, dirt brown) table cloth out there on the prairie.

Strawberry Dumplings
(adapted from a description by
Mary Powers, 1856)
Wet up some light dough and roll it
out with a bottle. Spread the berries
over it and roll it up in a cloth and boil
it. Make a cup full of sauce with the
juice of the berries and a little sugar
and nutmeg. Serve the sauce over the
dumplings.[3]

> Done some washing and I baked
> bread and pumpkin and apple pies
> cooked beans and meat stewed apples
> and baked suckeyes in quantitys
> sufficient to last some time—Besides
> making dutch cheese and took every
> thing out of the waggons to air . . .[4]
> —Cecelia Adams, 1852

Even prepared meals could suddenly disappear. Kit Belknap's party met Oregon pioneer and mountain man Joe Meek returning to Washington, DC to plead protection for the new Oregon settlers following the 1847 massacre of missionaries Narcissa and Marcus Whitman. "They had traveled all winter and some of their men had died," she wrote, "and they had got out of food and had to eat mule meat so we gave them all their supper and breakfast."

Dismayed at having to share scarce provisions, she wrote, "they made way with most all my stuff I had cooked up; on the whole we are having quite a time."

Author and historian Sandra L. Myres in *Westering Women* quoted a woman's dismay when a sandstorm hit her prepared dinner:

> After it was over our most intimate
> friends could hardly have recognized
> us—so dirty were our faces. And our
> dinner! Who would have eaten it? We
> could not tell what it consisted of,
> although before the storm it looked
> very tempting. So we had to cook
> another.[5]

Buffalo could be a hazard too. Those huge hairy beasts roamed the country along the Platte River, constantly on the move. You had to be watchful. They could tear through a camp in a big brown wave and scatter your livestock, flatten tents, and crush people beneath their powerful hooves.

But, the buffalo sustained life. In fact, author Irene Paden wrote that buffalo "made the emigration possible." As more emigrants would crowd onto the trail, there wouldn't be a stick of wood for days or weeks. The buffalo could provide a constant, renewable source of fuel for cooking food and warming the body.

The English Sportsman in the Western Prairies (1861)
by Grantley Berkeley
Courtesy of the National Historic Oregon Trail
Interpretive Center, Baker City, OR

In polite company, the emigrants would call it *bois de vache*, buffalo chips or meadow muffins. Other names for it were not for delicate ears. Whatever they called it, the plain fact was that their lives would depend on buffalo manure. Women and children would gather the chips, saving them in bags or aprons as they walked along beside the wagons. The first ones there would get the choicest chips: old enough not to be wet and stinky, fresh enough to provide substance for fuel. Some women would find another use for the stuff: as an "excellent mosquito repellent."

"[F]or the first time we cooked supper on buffalo chips," wrote Agnes Stewart as her party traveled along the Platte River Road in 1853. "[S]uch a use I would rather have wood but cannot get it."

Kit Belknap never mentioned cooking with buffalo chips. Perhaps she avoided the subject because the whole idea was so repugnant to her. After all, she was one who worked so hard at bringing home with her that she frequently mentioned table cloths, clean clothes, and ironing.

She did, however, write about the buffalo meat from a "nice young heifer" the men killed. "It is very coarse and dark meat but when cooked right made a very good change," she wrote.

Buffalo meat could be fried, boiled, put in "emigrant stew," or jerked—preserved for eating when food would be scarce.

Buffalo Jerky
Cut the meat into thin strips. Dip the strips in brine. Make a scaffold over a fire by putting forked sticks in the ground and laying straight sticks over them. Place the buffalo strips over the scaffold to dry for several hours. Or you can hang the strips from inside from the wagon bows. Or attach them to ropes reaching from front to back outside along the sides of the wagon. They will look something like red fringe and in the parched air, will dry out and provide food you can carry for a long distance without it spoiling.

The emigrants would find food sources along the way like wild onions and berries, and assorted animals like antelope, deer, rabbit, badger, prairie dog, sage hen, fresh water clams, and fish. In extreme circumstances, they would resort to eating dog, oxen, their own cows, and field mice.

In 1846, Ellen Smith trudged the last part of the way with eight of her children after her husband and one child died. Food and provisions were gone, and the children would go "out in the woods and smoke the Wood mice out of the Logs and Rost and Eat them."

Many women reported encounters with crickets, and their amazement at Indians' use of them:

> **The Crickets are large often an inch and a half or two inches in length— Black & shiney, the Indians make soup of them—They catch them by driving them into pits dug for this purpose— they are dried for winter use, its laughable to see our White Chickens try to swallow them, it often takes two or three efforts to get one disposed of, they are so numerous that one cannot avoid stepping on them.[6]**
>
> —Harriet Talcott Buckingham, 1851

Cooking would become more difficult as the emigrants would confront more hostile country, little water, and exhaustion of body, soul and supplies. Some would have to abandon their prized stoves and some, their Dutch ovens. Most would dig trenches for cooking, often with air tunnels to keep the fire going. Pots would be suspended from improvised scaffolds, placed on rocks over the fire, or on iron bars placed over the trenches.

On flue dug in the ground we coffee
  boild
And cooked our bacon, beans and rice;
And soon to our "hardtack" got
  reconciled
Where baking was not done at any
  price.
—Mrs. S. Watson Hamilton
"Pioneer of Fifty-Three"

When no wood or buffalo chips could be found, they would use anything that would burn, including sage.

For some, food would become scarce, and so would good water. "Oh how I long for a good drink of pure water," wrote Harriet Talcott Buckingham. Even when available, the water could carry deadly poison or disease. Women were finicky about drinking water and, according to author Irene Paden, refused to drink water with "wiggle-tails" in it. So they would kill the critters by boiling the water for coffee or tea, unknowingly killing deadly germs as well. Too often, they would drink water unboiled.

On a long, dry stretch in Wyoming, Kit Belknap wrote:

We will leave the sweet water in the
morning and have a long dry drive. Will
fill our kegs and everything that will
hold water so we will not suffer of
thirst. . . . I have a little water left yet;
will have to let the thirsty ox drivers
wet their parched lips. . . . We eat a
bite and go to bed.

Jackson's Panorama

Ruth and I stop for a drink of water from our plastic jug at a place called Jackson's Panorama, named for the famous landscape painter who captured scenes from the westward migration. One of his most famous paintings depicts the scene from about this spot in western Nebraska.

It must have been an eerie sight to the travelers. Stretching ahead are the three landmarks rising above the endless plains: Courthouse Rock, Chimney Rock, Scotts Bluff.

I step a few yards off the highway to get a photograph. The ground looks hard, but with each step, my sneakers sink at least an inch into the dust. Back in the car, I attack the thistles stuck in my socks and jeans, even my dusty sneakers. Some thorns are so stubborn I have to use the tweezers from my Swiss army knife to get them out.

Is this the kind of dusty, thorny country the women trudged through for hundreds of miles? In long cotton skirts? If those burrs tore into my jeans in just a few steps, what did they do to the women's dresses?

Many women would optimistically begin the journey wearing pretty dresses, cuffed and collared in white. It wouldn't be long before the white would turn brown and the pretty dress would be in tatters or left somewhere on the trail in a discarded trunk. A white, ironed apron would be more than an accessory. Washed frequently, it would cover dirt and remind its wearer of home.

"As the days lengthened into weeks, our self-respect suffered somewhat in the matter of clothes," wrote one woman. All that was left of her skirt was "a piece of wide fringe hanging from belt to hem."[7]

Parthenia Blank wrote of another trail hazard on her 1852 journey:

> **Last night my clothes got out of the wagon & the oxen eat them up & I consider I have met with a great loss as it was my woolen dress . . .**

Women would find that long, dark-colored linsey-woolsey homespun dresses would hold up best

National Historic Oregon Trail Interpretive Center
Baker City, OR

through the journey, offering some protection from the sun and wind and dust.

The long skirts would drag the ground, brush dangerously near the cooking fires or wagon wheels, and gather dust and mud and rips and tears. Yet the women wore them. Their long skirts were part of who they were. Practicality was quite irrelevant.

> **. . . the wind blows very hard that is reason it is so unpleasant for those who wear skirts . . .**
>
> —Agnes Stewart,
> after climbing
> Independence Rock, 1853

The Cult of Domesticity, which demanded that women be keepers of home and family while deferring to their husbands' supposedly superior intelligence and physical strength, dictated women's dress code. A True Woman was to be pale and modest. So she covered herself to avoid sunburn or tan and public scorn. A True Woman was not even supposed to reveal that she had two legs. So she covered her legs with long, cumbersome skirts and referred to legs as "limbs." She wouldn't think of riding a horse astride or shortening her skirts or—worst of all—wearing pants.

But for three years in the mid-nineteenth century, a few women would blaze a brave trail for freedom from long, cumbersome skirts—urban women, farm women, and some on the westward trails. Jane Kellogg wrote of her 1852 journey that "we wore bloomers all the way, the better to enable us to walk through the sagebrush. They were made with short skirts and pants reaching to the shoe tops. Everyone wore them."[8]

The flame of dress reform that burned as bright as a skirt aflame from a camp fire soon died. Mary Stewart Warner wrote in 1853 that she was brave enough to cross the plains but not brave enough to wear bloomers. Even the radical, valiant New York feminist Elizabeth Cady Stanton retreated to long skirts after three years of humiliation and ridicule from public critics and even her own family.

And yet. Long skirts served a highly useful purpose out there on the plains: the problem of taking care of daily bodily needs. With their skirts fanned out, women would provide "curtains of modesty" for other women to hide behind and take care of their bodily functions. Since few women wore underwear, skirts would be much handier than bloomers for such needs. The common ailment on the trail—diarrhea—would increase the urgency for ease and speed in such matters.

Women and girls would protect their faces from the sun and wind with the familiar bonnets. Esther Lockhart wrote in 1851 about the "slatted sun-bonnets" that were like the ones many women wore on the farm back home. The bonnets usually were made of gingham or seersucker of dark hues. "Rarely did we see any bright colors . . . Flaming colors would not have been considered modest then."[9] The bonnet's "bill" could measure up to ten inches, kept stiff with strips of light wood inserted into the layered cloth.

Women could fold the bonnets, and they could remove the wood strips ("slats") when they washed the bonnets, "which was not very often." A cape of fabric hung down from the lower part of the bonnet, protecting the woman's neck. "These old-fashioned sunbonnets may not have been beautiful, but they were a godsend to women on that long journey . . ."

Each traveler would require two or three changes of clothing. Men and women would wear cowhide boots. Boots would last for perhaps 300 miles, so one pair wouldn't be enough. Some wrote about going barefoot on the trail, even in the snow.

Mary Frances Scott traveled the trail with her family in 1852. At Fort Hall her shoes gave out and she had to cover her feet with wrappings. Much later, at The Dalles on the Columbia River, her father bought her new shoes. "These were the first shoes that I had to wear after my old pair wore out at Fort Hall," she remembered many years later.[10]

Men and boys would protect their faces from the sun and dust with big-brimmed felt or straw hats. Kerchiefs would be versatile and necessary for protection from wind and dust, and for protecting their necks from rough linsey-woolsey shirt collars, according to Bill Bullard of the National Frontier Trails Center. "Virtually everyone wore kerchiefs."

Women would wear scarves around their necks for protection from the elements, and to keep sweat from running down into their dresses.

> **. . . the sand reflecting back the heat of the sun in your face and makeing the swet trickle down oh this is going to origon . . .**
> —Helen Stewart, 1853

Unforeseen danger lurked in the great clouds of alkali dust in the Wyoming and Idaho high deserts. "Many emigrants had serious eye problems and suffered permanent damage from the dust," says Bullard. "Eye goggles would have been among their most important items, yet almost none of the emigrants had them."

That's not all they wouldn't have. It is a bitter irony that while women devoted meticulous care to preparing for the journey, they would ignore their own needs for warm clothing in the drenching rains, night freezes and mountain snows they would surely face in the last half of their trek.

"The home-manufactured clothing for women and children was frequently inadequate for the volatile weather on the trail," according to John Mack Faragher. Women sewed warm and somewhat waterproof coats for the men, Faragher found, but only shawls or light jackets to protect themselves. Was it a question of not having enough room to provide warm jackets for everyone? Did the women think they would be safe inside a warm wagon while the men were out in the weather?

. . . yesterday was a windy cold day I had to walk to keep myself warm and going about with a blanket round me it was hard to tell me from an Indian . . .
—Agnes Stewart, 1853

The children and myself are shivering round and in the wagons, nothing for fires in these parts, and the weather is very disagreeable.
—Amelia Stewart Knight, 1853

I used to wonder why it was said
man must be dressed in buckskin to
come to this country but now I know.
evry thing we travle through is thorny
and rough there is no chance of saving
your cloths here . . .
—Elizabeth Smith Geer, 1847

The woman facing westward with endless thorny and rough country ahead. I wonder. Will she ever wonder if perhaps a woman or a child should be dressed in buckskin too?

CHAPTER FIVE

The Journey: Where Is Home?

> As [my sister] with the other friends
> turned to leave me for the ferry which
> was to take them back to home and
> civilization, I stood alone on that wild
> prairie. . . .
> Looking westward I saw my husband
> driving slowly over the plain; turning
> my face once more to the east, my dear
> sister's footsteps were fast widening the
> distance between us. For the time I
> knew not which way to go, nor whom
> to follow. But in a few moments I
> rallied my forces. . . . and soon
> overtook the slowly moving oxen who
> were bearing my husband and child
> over the green prairie.[1]
> —Lavinia Porter, 1860

Which way does she go? How can she go? How
can she not go?

The words of historian and author Lillian
Schlissel come back to me: "Women are said to be
the middle rung between past and future," she told
me. "They are Janus-faced." I remember that Janus
was the Roman god with two faces, one looking
forward to the future, one looking backward to the
past.

Janus Head,
   ancient stone carving
Maryhill Museum
Goldendale, WA

Looking forward to a long journey and a new life, and backward to the home and family left behind, she moves westward.

Her ironed and starched white apron in place, she cuddles her infant in her arms and takes her place on the wagon seat. Her husband takes his place walking beside the wagon, driving the oxen.

> **. . . we present a sight we watched the cattle with a whip the men folks are yokeing up the oxen some packing up the wagons . . . what awkward attempt some of them do make at yoke oxen they never saw cattle scarcely before they started on this journey some swearing I think they might do without that sinning their souls for no end.**
> **—Agnes Stewart, 1853**

All manner of pots and pans and equipment dangle from the wagon bows. Chicken coops piggyback on the tail gate. We can imagine that with the plodding of the animal hooves, the creaking of the wagon, men hollering "gee" and "haw" at the oxen and cracking their whips, children crying, chickens protesting their cages, and pots and pans banging with the bumps, the wagon procession is anything but quiet.

Bouncing on the wagon seat, swaying slowly from side to side, the woman catches the look on her husband's face. She's never seen that look before. There's the confident walk, the determined set of his chin as he directs the oxen, but his eyes—a tightening in his eyes as he glances in her direction. Is he scared too? She longs to ask him, but now is not the time. Maybe tomorrow. But she knows tomorrow will be the same. Voicing her fears to him would only bring on a sharp response and a retreat to that determined set of chin. So she smiles at him, then turns to her diary to confide her fears.

> **Shall we all reach the "Eldorado" of our hopes, or shall one of our number be left, and our graves be in the dreary wilderness, our bodies uncoffined, and unknown remain there in solitude.**
> —Elizabeth Goltra, 1853

While I try to imagine what must be going through the mind of a woman beginning her westward journey, words from a woman's diary circle my mind:

> **The heart has a thousand misgivings.**

Does she know she likely won't be sitting on that seat for most of the journey? She'll have to walk much of the way, maybe even most of the way. The lurching of the wagon over rocks and gulleys and hills and cruel descents will make riding impossible much of the time. Later on, her added weight will be a burden to the oxen whose strength will be spent—if they're alive at all.

In my car, beginning my journey to Independence and back, I mentally reviewed my checklist of essentials: cameras, film, batteries, portable computer, notebooks, pens, guidebooks, address book, credit cards, cash. Important stuff, yes. Others would provide food and shelter for me along the way, and I could replace anything I needed along the road.

The woman facing westward knows that one mistake, one item forgotten or overlooked could make the difference between reaching the destination or facing death along the way.

She thinks:

Have I forgotten anything? Do we have the right medicine? Enough food? Is the wagon strong enough to make the trip? Will we find food for the animals? Will the children be warm enough? Does Husband have enough ammunition to protect us from dangers along the way? Will I ever see my mother again?

And the child growing in my body. Where will we be when the babe comes? Will it be in a storm? Will I have a woman to help me? Will it die? Will I die?

Will my family make it? And if we do, what will be there for us?

Is this all a mistake?

Is it too late to turn back?

*And yet—we'll work hard, have our own land,
and not be sick so much. We'll build schools and
churches and make another home. Like the one we
left. Must turn my attention to the present. Hold the
family together.*

The heart has a thousand misgivings—so
profound they can't even find their way into a
diary.

> **little one crying with cold feet**
> **sixteen wagons all getting ready to**
> ** cross the creek**
> **hurry and bustle and get breakfast over**
> **feed the cattle**
> **and tumble things into the wagons**
> **hurrah boys all ready**
> **we will be the first to cross the creek**
> ** this morning**
> **gee up Tip and Tyler [names of oxen]**
> **and away we go**
> **the sun just rising**
> —Amelia Stewart Knight, 1853

Amelia Stewart Knight, with her husband and
their seven children, left their Iowa home in their
oxen-drawn wagons on an early April day that
turned into a "cold and frosty" night. By the second
day, rains soaked the family, two children had the
mumps, and the "poor cattle bawl all night." By the
seventh day:

> **. . . every body out of humour,**
> **Seneca is half sick, Plutarch has broke**
> **his saddle girth, Husband is scolding,**
> **and hurriing all hands (and the cook)**
> **and Almira says She wishes she was**
> **home, and I say ditto, Home sweet**
> **home . . .**

A week later, and they haven't even crossed the Missouri yet:

> **Dreary times, wet and muddy, and
> crowded into the tent, cold and wet and
> uncomfortable in the wagon no place
> for the poor children, I have been busy
> cooking, roasting coffe &c to day, and
> have came into the wagon to write this
> and make our bed—**

Most emigrants traveled to a jumping-off place like Independence (in the early years) or St. Joseph or Kanesville (Council Bluffs) in their wagons. Some brought their supplies by steamboat and bought their wagons and supplies there at the jumping-off place. To men, those jumping-off places were exciting and colorful. For many women, they were disappointing.

> **Arrived at St. Joseph today. Was
> quite disappointed at the appearance of
> the place. I had expected to find
> nothing but log cabins and frame
> shantys, instead found brick houses and
> plenty of whiskey shops and every man
> I meet looks [as] if they where an ale
> cask themselves. To my opinion St.
> Joseph would rise a great deal faster if
> the people here did not take so much
> advantage of the emigrants . . .**
> **   —Agnes Stewart, 1853**

Even to get to the jumping-off place, travelers might face late spring storms, cholera, food shortages and drowning at river crossings. Despite doubts and hardships, a mood of optimism propelled the emigrants facing the unknown distance for the promised land of Oregon.

I am bound for the promised land
I'm bound for the promised land
O who will come and go with me
I am bound for the promised land

—spiritual

We read the women's words and listen for their voices. We see many-hued patchworks of individual lives bound together by the common bonds of tradition and determination to remember the fabric of home and community and carry it with them.

the prairie is our table
the prairie is our bed
the prairie is our chair
our home tilts and slants
over open fields

—from *Pioneer Woman*
©1979 by Pat McMartin Enders

Most women who traveled the trail were mothers or soon to be mothers. It was the mothers who, more than anyone, looked both forward and back, remembering home and how it was made. It was the mothers who tried to stretch the protective fabric of home across the 2,000 miles to a new place.

It strikes me as I think of it now that
Mothers on the road had to undergo
more trial and suffering than anybody
else.²

—Martha Ann Morrison,
age thirteen in 1844

I've often been asked if we did not
suffer with fear in those days but I've
said no we did not have sense enough
to realize our danger we just had the

National Historic
Oregon Trail
Interpretive Center
Baker City, OR

**time of our lives but since I've grown
older and could realize the danger and
the feelings of the mothers, I often
wonder how they really lived through it
all and retained their reason.**[3]
—Nancy Hembree Snow Bogart, 1845

As they did on the farm, the women and the men
kept their separate cultures—at least in the
beginning until the going got much tougher and
survival was at stake. Some tasks were easier or
non-existent on the trail: no house to clean,
although it was no small chore to keep some
semblance of order in the wagon; little or no
ironing, although some women insisted on ironing
clothes far into the trek; no crops to weed and
harvest.

But in trying to bring home with them, the
women—like the men—had to learn whole new
sets of skills: cooking outdoors, trying to keep
things dry, coping with vicious weather, struggling

with sickness and child birth while on the move, walking mile after mile in heat or cold or snow or dust, harnessing and driving the oxen, bartering with Indians and mountain men for food and supplies.

Child care was a frightening task. Simply dealing with normal childhood fretfulness was trying, as one mother noted: "I am going to get some switches as the boys are crying. They have driven me almost crazy."[4]

Dangers lurked everywhere for children: getting lost, getting left, falling under wheels, falling ill, drowning at river crossings, getting into firearms or deadly medicines, cold and hunger and sickness.

> **Then cholera took my oldest boy**
> **His sister Isabel fell beneath the wagon**
> **And was crushed beneath the wheels.**
> —from "Overland 1852"

Keeping some sense of cleanliness was next to impossible. How do you get your clothes and dishes and your face clean when there's no clean water? Those with foresight took only dark-colored linens and aprons on the trail—ones that wouldn't show the dirt. Using multi-purpose kettles, the women would boil water for the wash when time allowed.

Most wagon trains had layover days, when women washed and baked and men hunted, repaired gear and sometimes even helped with the wash. Men, the decision makers, might refuse to stop for needs to wash and bake or tend the sick or bury the dead or wait for slower companions, but they were inclined to stop everything for the hunt.

John Mack Faragher, in *Women and Men on the Overland Trail*, noted that "despite expert advice as to the folly of stopping the march for a hunt, men who otherwise stressed the importance of continual movement above all else would stop their wagons, saddle all available mounts, and head out for the kill at the slightest sign of a distant buffalo herd."

For many women, part of bringing home with them was honoring the Sabbath. Not stopping and resting on the Sabbath was a distressing sign that civilization was unraveling, but necessity dictated that the travelers either work on the Sabbath or keep moving.

> . . . this is sabath . . . take
> everything out of our wagon to air them
> and it is well we done it as the flower
> [flour] was damp . . . and we baked
> and boiled and washed oh dear me I did
> not think we would haved abuse the
> sabeth in such a manner I do not see
> how we can expect to get along but we
> did not intend to do so before we
> started . . .
>
> —Helen Stewart, 1853

The women discovered that if the Sabbath was kept for a day of rest, too often, rest was only for the men. "Sabbath was made for men," one woman complained to her diary.

Besides the elusive day of rest and meditation, women missed the social aspect of Sunday worship, with communal singing and meditation. One man recalled a woman sadly singing alone on a Sunday evening:

> The sound of the church-going bell
> These valleys and rocks never heard;
> Ne'er sighed at the sound of a knell,
> Or smiled when a Sabbath appeared.[5]

Helen Stewart's diary reflected not only the disruption of the Sabbath but of sex roles when she wrote,

I wish I could go to meating some place but in stead of that I mount a horse and help to drive the lose cattle.

Another fear—encounters with Indians—was generally unfounded, at least in early years. In the beginning, fear of Indians translated to stark prejudice as time after time women described them as dirty and lazy. Later, fear of the dreaded Indians often turned to curiosity, even admiration.

Most of the males had no clothing but a sort of apron. They are the most pleasant agreeable looking indians I have ever seen.

—Celinda Hines, 1853

National Historic
Oregon Trail
Interpretive
Center
Baker City, OR

In the early migration years, Indians were more intent on trading and seeing if they could get away with white men's prized horses than in getting away with their scalps, as Amelia Stewart Knight discovered:

I was very much frightened while at this camp, and lie awake all night—I expected every minite we would all be killed, however we all found our scalps on in the morning.

It was in the later years—after the mid-1850s—
that the dangers from Indian attack were real.
Indians struck back in desperation after the stream
of intruders brought death and disease and destruction to the land that was their home.

As Ruth and I drive along the freeway that now
blankets the Oregon Trail, we look for the tall grass
like the kind pictured in the National Frontier
Trails Center, with the Indian standing on his horse
to see over the grass. Now, there's no tall grass,
except for places like the Flint Hills National
Wildlife Refuge south of Topeka.

It's hard to visualize what it was like because you
have to try to place your imagination under the
cultivated fields, roads, fences and highways that
now crisscross the country where once tall grass
grew, and hardly any trees. After the emigrants
came through, pioneers settled here and planted
groves of trees on the prairies to recreate the treed
landscapes of their homes farther east.

We notice the patches of wildflowers where once
they covered the landscape, inviting women and
children to pick them and brighten their portable
homes.

To the emigrants, the pleasant landscape looked
deceptively safe. The tranquil scene could suddenly
turn into a savage place as spring storms struck,
leaving flattened tents, wet people and clothes and
food, even overturned wagons. Frightened livestock
would take off across the plains, creating chaos—
sometimes stampedes—stealing valuable time
rounding them up again.

*Where is protection when the sky opens up and
shoots big, white bullets at you and tears up your
home? Where can you hide?*

. . . we had a dreadful storm of rain
and hail last night, and very sharp
lightning, it killed 2 oxen for one man
. . . every brute was gone out of sight,
cows, calves, horses all gone before the
storm like so many wild beasts. . . .
[T]he rain beat into the wagons so that
every thing was wet, and in less than
two hours, the water was a foot deep all
over our camping ground . . . all hands
had to crowd into the wagons and sleep
in wet beds, with their wet clothes on,
without supper . . .
          —Amelia Stewart Knight, 1853

Platte River

The wagon procession reaches the Platte—the
wide, flat cottonwood-lined river that ambles across
Nebraska and reaches clear into Wyoming. The
woman facing ever westward is probably walking
most of the time now, gathering buffalo chips for
the camp fire instead of wildflowers for her home.

By now, most wagon trains would have elected
leaders. Candidates would take off across the

prairie and other men would follow, lining up behind their favorite. The one with the longest line would win.

This practice had its roots in the Midwestern tradition of "muster day," according to historian John Mack Faragher. Using the pretext of practicing "drills," the muster was an opportunity for male camaraderie and its accompanying singing, wrestling, fighting, racing, and gambling. The mustering men would elect their officers by lining up behind their choice.

At Ash Hollow, they stare down a long hill they call Windlass Hill. Instructions for negotiating it might look something like this [adapted from Kit Belknap and others]:

> **Take one wagon at a time as far as you can with the team. Then unhitch and ruff-lock both hind wheels [slide a tree or pole through the wheels to lock them]. Then fasten a big rope to the axles of the wagon. The men will hold to the rope to keep the wagon iron from going end over end. Women can brake the wagon by placing big stones in front of the wheels. Some men will be at the tongue to steer the wagon and others will lift the wheels to ease them down the steps for it is solid rock steps from six inches to two feet part. This can take all day but you can get through without accident.**

The Platte River Road and beyond became a litter path, a grave yard, a trail of oxen bones. Some said you could smell your way to Oregon from the stench of dead oxen and find your way by the litter and the graves.

I measured each day's progress
by the miles and by the graves
And the fear that gripped my heart
I will remember all my days.
                    —"Overland 1852"

On the bluffs above the Platte
you can look back at the wide seas
of grass sloping this way and that,
at the wide, dry sea of America
strewn with the discards: food,
bedding, clothes, trunks full
of ball dresses, books, furniture,
machinery—everything, in fact.
                    —from *Pioneer Woman*

They had to do it. Time was growing short and
the oxen were growing weak. They had to lighten
their load. Each discarded rocking chair, each
abandoned trunk, each deserted toy told a story of
someone leaving part of themselves behind there
on the lonely prairie.

A box full of ribbons, a toy soldier's
    drum
And the old chair of mama's she rocked
    in the sun,
The cradle abandoned is still on my
    mind.
I'm afraid I'm still missing what we left
    behind.

This table's too heavy, this mirror's
    been cracked
And this old chest of grandpa's will just
    hold us back
Oh, this trail's lined with pieces from
    long ago times
I'm afraid I'm still missing what we left
    behind.

And I'm not afraid of lightning, or the
    wolf at my door,
And I'm not afraid of dying all alone
    any more, but when
Journeys are over and there's fruit on
    our vine, I'm afraid I'll
Be missing what we left behind.
        —"What We Left Behind"
    ©1991 by Marv Ross, Troutdog Music

Women turned to one another to share laughter and hope, and to ease the hardship and the pain. As they walked together ever westward,

   . . . we womenfolk visited from
wagon to wagon or congenial friends
spent an hour walking . . . and talking
over our home life back in 'the states';
telling of the loved ones left behind;
voicing our hopes for the future . . .
and even whispering a little friendly
gossip of emigrant life.[6]
        —Catherine Haun, 1849

The communities of women often cooked together, sometimes swam together, and exchanged "receipts" as they knitted, sewed new dresses or desperately-needed moccasins, mended tattered clothes, crocheted and pieced quilt tops. In time of disaster, birth and death, the women came together in time-honored circles of understanding and comfort and help.

Separation on the trail from other women and their companionship was one of the tragedies of the Oregon Trail. The worst way for a woman to travel was only in the company of men. Who could she express her fears and feelings to? How would she take care of personal needs without the shield of other women's skirts? Who would help her when it was time for her child to be born?

Close your eyes as you ride the wagon pulled by ropes across the river. Hang tight to the children.

> **Old Noah, he built himself an ark,**
> **There's one more river to cross.**
> **He built it out of hickory bark,**
> **There's one more river to cross.**
> **There's one more river,**
> **And that's the river of Jordan.**
> **There's one more river,**
> **Just one more river to cross.**
>   —"One More River to Cross"
>   popular camp song

Lucia Loraine Williams recalled a harrowing river crossing in 1851:

> **[A]n old lady who was badly**
> **frightened came over to our wagon and**
> **asked permission to ride with us for**
> **awile. She said, 'It looks like you gals**
> **never git scairt. You jest set thar with**
> **your sewin' or your knittin' just as**
> **though nothin' had happened.'**[7]

The quilts brought from home warmed their bodies, cradled treasures, and lined wagons. Quilts could provide a quick cover for exposed sides of wagons in case of Indian attacks. Too often, heartbroken emigrants used quilts as burial cloths along the trail.

An 1849 diary described the burial cloths of a mother and her infant on the desert

> . . . in this weird, lonely spot on God's footstool away apparently from everywhere and everybody.
>
> The bodies were wrapped together in a bed comforter and wound, quite mummified with a few yards of string that we made by tying together torn strips of a cotton dress skirt.[8]
>
> —Catherine Haun, 1849

Sanitation on the trail was even worse than it had been on the farm. Water supplies and cooking mixed with milling animals and their waste. As on the farm, the emigrants used common drinking cups. Especially in heavy migration years, crowding on the trail quickly polluted springs and shallow drinking holes along the way. Water sources became perfect breeding grounds for infectious diseases—typhoid, tuberculosis, malaria, dysentery, pneumonia, measles, smallpox, yellow fever, and—worst of all—cholera.

The heart has a thousand misgivings . . .

> Cholera wears a black feather, and the graves become shallower where wolves learn the art of looting.
>
> —from *Pioneer Woman*

Cholera could strike so quickly there would be hardly time to say good-bye. Hardly time to bury the loved one. Must move on. Drive the wagon over the grave. Maybe the wolves can't find her under the hard-packed trail.

Sisters Abigail (Duniway) and Catherine Scott (Coburn) crossed the plains with their parents, brothers and sisters in 1852. Two months after their mother died of cholera, their beloved four-year-old brother died on the trail. Thirteen-year-old Catherine described her brother's death in a letter to her Grandfather:

National Historic
Oregon Trail
Interpretive Center
Baker City, OR

   . . . our dear little Willie was taken
sick with Direah . . . he could not
speak for several days before he died
but would take a cup and hold it out for
water was the only sign he would
make, after nine days sickness he died
leaving us in a wild desert place to
mourn over him he is buried on the
side of a hill under a lone cedar tree on
Burnt river.

In a later poem, seventeen-year-old Abigail expressed the agony of watching the death of a "brother most dear/Whose eyeballs are frightfully swimming in death . . ."

Crossing the Black Hills of what is now Wyoming, you walk. The boulders jutting out of this crude path they call a road jar the wheels and the bones. The sights and smells offend the senses.

> **. . . well well people talk of being in mud to the eyes but if we have not got dust to our eyes it is a strange thing to me not withstanding we could not walk for dung and could not breath for the smell of dead oxen . . .**
>
> —Agnes Stewart, 1853

> **We saw whitening on the plains, bones of animals which had died on the way.**[9]

Whitening on the plains is still there on the sagebrush prairies. It's from the alkali—both friendly and deadly to the emigrant trains. The white substance permeates the water, and when the water evaporates, the white remains, forming ominous patches of white across the prairies.

Women often called the alkali "saleratus," an old term for baking soda, and they did gather the alkali deposits for baking.

> **. . . this saleratus is far from being equeal to artificial saleratus although**

Alkali in Wyoming

**looks as good we got a great deal of it
some kep and used it others threw it
away it will not foam buter milk one
bit . . . we at rising this morning baked
a lot of light bread moved on . . .**
—Elizabeth Dixon Smith, 1847

An animal drinking alkali water could be dead
the same day. Through cracked lips, chapped from
the parched, windy weather, the men yelled at the
animals to stay away from that water. Some even
had to beat the animals to keep them from drinking
the water that could kill them.

**. . . had a great deal of trouble to
keep the stock from drinking the
poision or alkali water, it is almost sure
to kill man or beast who drink it . . .**
—Amelia Stewart Knight, 1853

Many women's diaries expressed concern for the gentle beasts that pulled their homes westward. They recorded both cruelty and gentleness toward the animals.

> **It's very warm; the oxen all have their tongues out panting. George took the wash pan and a bucket of water and let all our team wet their tongues and he washed the dust off their noses; some laughed at him but the oxen seemed very grateful.**
>
> —Kit Belknap, 1848

Some emigrants treated alkali-poisoned oxen with hot grease.

> **This morning our cattle and horses are all sick, we found we had camped on alkali ground, we commenced pouring the lard and vinegar down them and they soon seemed better, drove on to get away from this poisonous place . . .**
>
> —Elizabeth Goltra, 1853

The dust. The wind blew the dust kicked up by the wagons and the animals' hooves. Alkali dust burned the skin and the animals' hooves, ate away at the emigrants' shoes and boots, and, worst of all, the eyes of people and animals alike.

> **. . . the boys have driven the cattle on to an Island where they can get gras, and I have just washed the dust out of my eyes so that I can see to get supper . . .**
>
> —Amelia Stewart Knight, 1853

The dry windy air attacked the wagons, splintering the wood and shrinking and loosening the wheels from their rims. Breakdowns added to the misery.

Watch for snakes. Cover your face against the dust. Where's the littlest one? You've heard about children wandering off and never coming back to you again.

A tumbleweed greets Ruth and me on cue as we cross the border into Wyoming. Our air conditioner cools us from the hot, heavy air. To the northwest, the skies billow smoke from distant fires. Suddenly, the air turns so cold that we switch to the heater within five minutes. Here, the weather can change that quickly.

Finally, they reach the friendly Sweetwater River—named for a lost pack of sugar. It greets the beaten-down travelers, offering safe, cool water and welcome shade.

Not far down the road is Independence Rock.

Celebrate! If you reach Independence Rock by July 4, you're making good time. Wade into the cool Sweetwater and wash the layers of dirt off your weary, smelly body. Wash your clothes in the river and dry them on the banks. Put on your best dress—the one that's still holding together, the one that wasn't left behind along the road.

**For your amusement I will give a
description of my dress for the**

occasion: A red calico frock, made for
the purpose in the wagons; a pair of
mockasins, made of black buffalo hide,
ornamented with silk insted of beads,
as I had none of the latter and a hat
braided, of bullrushes and trimmed
with white, red and pink ribbon and
white paper. I think I came pretty near
looking like a squaw.[10]

—Elizabeth Wood, 1851

*Break out the spirits! Feast on the food you've
been saving up for this celebration!*

**Menu for Independence Day
(adapted from Lorena Hayes and
Wells West, 1853)[11]**
quite a number of kinds of cake
preserves
pies
butter, cheese
sauce
rice, beans
sausages, ham
biscuit
tea, coffee &c
fruit cake baked back home in Illinois
    and saved for the celebration

*Bring out the fiddles! Forget what the preachers
told you about dancing your way to hell! The rules
are different here. Dance on the prairie!*

As I was goin' down the road
a tired team an' a heavy load
I crack'd my whip and the leader
    sprung and says,
day-day, to the wagon tongue.

Turkey in the straw, turkey in the hay
dance all night and work all day
Roll 'em up and twist 'em up a high,
    tuck-a-haw
and hit 'em up a tune call'd Turkey in
    the Straw.

—popular trail song

    . . . this is the fourth in the States a
great many . . . is prepareing for
pleasure of some kind but we are
selerabrating it by traviling in sand and
dust but we had a great dance tonight
. . . I went up on the hill and talked
over old times . . . and then we come
down and danced untill neerly one
oclock it done very well for want of
better fun it is a beautiful eavening the
star shine bright we have excelent grass

—Helen Stewart, 1853

There were good times to be had on the Oregon
Trail—most often for the young and unattached:
picking wildflowers, swimming in a stream, nur-
turing new friendships, discovering new skills like
horseback riding, and, of course, music and
dancing.

Some lucky travelers still had their musical
instruments with them.

We are a merry crowd, while I am
journalizeing one of the company is
playing the violin which sounds

**delightful way out here. My accordian
is also good, as I carry it in the carrige
and play as we travel . . .**[12]
                    —Amelia Hadley, 1851

*Move on. Past Devil's Gate. Aptly named. In this
country, the heat can reach over 100 degrees in the
day and chill the bones at night.*
Move on. You're not even halfway there.

South Pass area, Wyoming

South Pass. Not what you'd picture as a
mountain pass. It's more like a wide saddle on the
endless horizon. The only way you can tell for sure
you've crossed the Continental Divide is that you're
now traveling downstream, not upstream as you've
been doing for the last 900 miles.

At South Pass, the hard part isn't getting over the
mountain. The hardest part is deciding which way
to go.

From here on are many cutoffs. Many temptations to cut short a trip that seems endless. Many reasons for changing your mind about where you're going. Many ways to get into more trouble.

**For two months we had traveled
and half our oxen dead
Our wagon being slow,
the others chose to go ahead**
                                        —"Overland 1852"

Stories of the trails west are stories of separation—separation from families and friends back home, separation by death, and separation by parting of the ways. Wagon trains regularly divided, with changes in plans, too much crowding, flaring tempers, the lure of an easier path. Sometimes travelers, in their hurry to beat bad weather and cholera, left others behind.

Elizabeth Stewart Warner crossed the plains from Pennsylvania in 1853 with her new husband, her sisters, including Agnes and Helen Stewart, and their parents. She recalled the agony of leaving behind another sister, whose heavily-loaded wagon couldn't keep up. Her account also captures the separation of women and men on the trail west.

**. . . one of stewart's [the sister's
husband] wagons broke down and wes
mended next day we had ben telling
him that he ought not to presist in
taking such big wagons but he would
no advice and . . . the men held a
council and determined not to wait for
him for they saw he would never keep
up. Our wemen protested against it but
they started and we were obliged to
follow. . . . it was best for us to go on
but it was hard to part I do not think**

**that Mother will ever get over it she
blames her self for not standing still
and she blames us for not doing the
same and she blames the men for
leaving them. mother says that no
consequence could never make her do
the like again.**

I think of Elizabeth and her sisters and mother
pulling into the wagon line, leaving the sister
behind. She knows they must keep moving ahead
as fast as they can. Yet she keeps looking back,
hoping to see her sister coming, knowing that she's
safe.

Elizabeth never did see her sister coming. Months
later, she would learn that her sister and family had
turned south and arrived safely in California.

At Old Fort Boise, the Stewarts left the trail to try
an untried cutoff to the west:

> **. . . parted our company yesterday
> The Stevensons and Buckinghams took
> the old road and Loves and Stewarts
> took the new one south from the old
> road some say it is much nearer some
> say not we will see soon . . .**
> —Agnes Stewart, 1853

The "new road" was one of many "new" routes
that appealed to the tired and increasingly-
desperate emigrants, thinking it would save time
and grief. It did not. Sisters Elizabeth, Agnes, and
Helen became part of the "Lost Wagon Train of
1853." Agnes and Helen stopped writing, and
Elizabeth would write later:

**. . . then we came to the new road
they talk about the times that tried men
souls but if this ware not the times that
tried both men and wemon's souls . . .**

Men argued over which way to go. Treatment of
animals, placement in line, women's affections,
general cussedness—all prompted quarrels and
sometimes violence. Some men clung to running
feuds the whole way.

Agnes Stewart wrote about a long-standing
quarrel between her sister Elizabeth's husband,
Fred, and the man Agnes would eventually marry:

**. . . today we had quarrel again and
as usual fred came to blows Tom and
he are always quarreling about
something I do wish they had never
come with us but it cannot be helped
now but it is very disagreeable for to
bear with them. Tom is impudent Fred
overbearing and arrogant and between
the two we have sorry time with
them . . .**

Abigail Scott Duniway wrote in a letter home
about a murder and trial on a wagon train from
Wisconsin and added:

**This is the ninth case of death by
violence on the route, three of whom
were executed, the others were
murdered This route is the greatest one
for wrangling, discord and abuse of any
other place in the world I am certain.**

What we now euphemistically call domestic
violence happened on the trail as well. Historians

don't agree on its frequency. Of the diaries I've read, seldom does a woman write about any violence done to her—it's always someone else. What really happened will probably never be known.

Kit Belknap wrote about a scene in the wagon next to hers:

> **She wants to turn back and he wont
> go so she says she will go and leave him
> with the children and he will have a
> good time with that crying baby, then
> he used some very bad words and said
> he would put it out of the way. Just
> then I heard a muffled cry and a heavy
> thud as tho something was thrown
> against the wagon box and she said 'Oh
> you've killed it' and he swore some
> more and told her to keep her mouth
> shut or he would give her more of the
> same.**

"The baby was not killed," Kit wrote, adding, "I write this to show how easy we can be deceived." What she meant and what really happened is not known.

Approaching Fort Hall in present-day Idaho, Kit Belknap's little boy is "very sick with Mountain Fever." Facing a "long dry drive" ahead, she "cooks up" provisions and fills every container with water, and they travel all night. Next morning she writes:

> **I have been awake all night watching
> with the little boy. . . . The sun is just**

**rising and it shows a lot of the dirtiest
humanity every was seen since the
Creation. We just stop for an hour and
eat a bite and let the teams breath
again. We divide the water with the
oxen. . . . I thot in the night we would
have to leave [the little boy] here and I
thot if we did I would be likely to stay
with him but as the daylight, we
seemed to get fresh courage.**

Traveling at night with weakened oxen over
country with no water and nursing a desperately
sick child, Kit Belknap faces the hardest part of the
journey—the deserts and mountains of what is now
Oregon. She has never mentioned that she is also
pregnant. Regrettably, though understandably, her
account of the journey ends here. She continues on,
bears her child in present-day eastern Oregon, and
settles in the Willamette Valley.

We have few accounts of pregnancy and childbirth from the women who traveled the trail. A
woman might write that she feels "sick" and then
suddenly a baby will appear. Some historians who
have contrasted original diaries with those
transcribed by families have discovered that the
families have censored out references to pregnancy
and sex! So between censorship of self and family,
such matters often have been left to the
imagination.

Martha Gay Masterson recalled a morning surprise on her 1851 trek when she was thirteen.

> **Early on the morning of June 14 I was awakened from a nervous sleep by the wailing of an infant. I asked mother whose baby was crying so. She said it was hers. I said not a word for some time, fearing I might have to welcome another brother. I already had nine brothers. I was so anxious to know I asked, "Is it a little brother?" Imagine my joy when she said it was a little sister. Then I hastily dressed and wanted to see it. I thought it surely was the cutest and sweetest little sister in all the wide world.[13]**

We can only imagine what it must have been like for a woman to bear a child—or for that matter, to become pregnant—on the Oregon Trail. Mother and child would be lucky to have a layover day. Often the train hardly stopped at all. Dirt and muck often surrounded the birth scene, putting their very lives in peril. Most deaths associated with childbirth resulted from germ-caused infection.

Medical doctors John A. Lavin and James A. McGregor, in their study of Plains Indians childbirth practices, wrote that American Indian women would not allow human touch of the birthing woman's pelvic area. This probably explains the Indian women's lower death rate for both mother and child in childbirth.

Historian Sandra L. Myres surmised that when water was scarce, emigrant women resorted to drying, scraping and airing precious diaper cloths and reused them until they could be washed. Imagine the problems with diaper rash—not to mention infection. According to Myres, some women may have followed the Indian women's practice of using grass or soft moss for "disposable diapers."

Women who were not pregnant had to cope with the problem of menstruation, although there is speculation that some may have stopped having periods because of the stress to their systems. Trying to be discreet about washing and applying menstrual cloths must have been mortifying for these women.

As she moves farther from all she has known and nearer her destination, she sees the fabric of home and the life she knew unraveling before her eyes.

**I must keep writing
to remember
who I am.**
—from *Pioneer Woman*

Where is home?

**The heart has a thousand misgivings,
and the mind is tortured with anxiety,
and often as I passed the fresh made
graves I have glanced at the side boards
of the wagons, not knowing how soon it
would serve as a coffin for some one of
us.**[14]
—Lodisa Frizzell, 1852

The Sabbath is no longer honored. She is doing things she never dreamed of—driving the oxen, trading with the Indians precious items from home for precious food, burying loved ones in a lonely land, wearing rags for clothes, yelling at her children and her husband, scrounging for food.

Barlow Road Soup
(adapted from Abigail Scott Duniway's
journal, 1852, on the Barlow Trail
in Oregon's Cascade Mountains)[15]
Boil an antiquated ham bone. Add to
the liquid the few scrapings from the
dough pan in which you mixed the
biscuit from your last measure of flour,
which by now will be musty and sour.
If you have no bone, thicken some
water from flour shaken from a
remaining flour sack.

Most women managed to "school in," as Agnes Stewart described it:

O I feel lonesome today sometimes I
can govern myself but not always but I
schooled in pretty well considering all
things.

She knows she has to hold in her fears and longings. If she ever starts to let them out, they may never stop. Then she'd be a carping wife, and maybe she'd simply go mad.

One of the most poignant examples of "schooling in" and letting it out was that of Lavinia Porter, who wrote of her 1860 journey:

I would make a brave effort to be
cheerful and patient until the camp
work was done. Then starting out

**ahead of the team and my men folks,
when I thought I had gone beyond
hearing distance, I would throw myself
down on the unfriendly desert and give
way like a child to sobs and tears,
wishing myself back home with my
friends and chiding myself for
consenting to take this wild goose
chase.**[16]

Diaries sometimes reflected unbelievable—almost comical—restraint. On her 1853 journey, Charlotte Pengra was driving the oxen because her husband was too ill to do it. She herself was ill, as was her child, and they had run out of meat and sugar.

"I am somewhat discouraged," she wrote, "and shall be glad when this journey is ended."

Later, separated from her larger family and alone with three men, Charlotte wrote, "I feel lonely and almost disheartened."

The "somewhat discouraged" and "almost disheartened" would on occasion explode into fits of anger and insurrection. There are accounts of women talking back to their husbands and throwing things at them, yelling at trail bosses, making demands at gun point, refusing to cook, refusing to camp in a chosen spot. Some decided what the hell and wore pants. Lavinia Porter drained her husband's whole barrel of whiskey.

Even the normally-restrained Kit Belknap got uppity. In a vague reference to her own "noteriety," she wrote:

**Watts and the sheep pulled out and
fell behind. I got the blame for the split.
The old Mother Watts said after they
got thru 'Yes, Geo. Belknaps' wife is a
little woman but she wore the pants on
that train' so I came into noteriety
before I knew it . . .**

Elizabeth Dixon Smith recorded in 1847 one of the most famous accounts of a woman's burst of anger on the Oregon Trail. The woman got mad, Elizabeth wrote, set fire to their wagon and told her husband she had "picked up a stone and nocked out [their son's] brains." The husband then "mustered spunk enough to give her a good floging."

It turns out the woman was Elizabeth Markham, who became Oregon's first woman writer[17] and mother of the famous poet Edwin Markham. She raised the boy single-handedly in California after she and her husband divorced.

In her published poem "Road to Oregon," Elizabeth Markham wrote:

> **Such clouds of mist hang round the scene,**
> **O'er which we have no control;**
> **It's like a half-remembered dream,**
> **Or tale that's long been told.**[18]

Despite the hardships and harshness, women wrote about acts of kindness—to family, friends and strangers alike. The father trudges through rain and mud to bring supplies and shoes for his daughters. Husbands and wives care for each other in sickness. Strangers share food. Indians ferry emigrants across rivers, bringing them salmon, showing them the way. A husband brings his wife flowers on the trail. People take in orphaned children.

Where is home?

Most had expected to be "home" by August. By October and even later, many are still making their way westward. As they enter what is now Oregon, they face the hardest part yet: more desert and treacherous mountains. When they reach the Columbia River, they must make a critical decision.

They can risk losing their remaining belongings and their lives floating the Columbia on rafts or Indian canoes. Or they can inch their way over yet another mountain range that's worse than any they've encountered so far, on a wretched trail drenched in rain, wallowing in mud and covered in snow in the highest places.

By now the woman is no longer looking backward. She's had to forget what she left behind back home and along the trail.

Her friends and family back home would hardly recognize her face. She has faced the unmerciful elements, disease, perhaps death and starvation. She has walked most of those 2,000 miles.

By the time she reaches her destination, she hardly recognizes herself. She knows she is not the same woman who left her home 2,000 miles away.

And she knows something else:

Did not want to camp out again.[19]
            —Lucia Loraine Williams, 1851

National Historic Oregon Trail Interpretive Center
Baker City, OR

CHAPTER SIX

The Promised Land:
Where Is Home?

The birds singing gaily,
    that came at my call;
Give me them, and that peace of mind,
    dearer than all.
Home! home! sweet, sweet home!
There's no place like home!

There's no place like home.
                    —"Home, Sweet Home"
                    by John Howard Payne

The woman has been facing westward, walking mostly, for two thousand miles of heat and dust and snow and rain and mud. It is September or October, maybe even December or January. She stopped looking back long ago. Now she looks only forward, to home.

Does the sun shine on her? Are the family and loved ones she left with still with her? Does she still have shoes on her feet? Is anyone there to welcome her home?

Where is home?

My most vivid recollection of that
first winter in Oregon is of the weeping
skies and of Mother and me also
weeping.[1]

                    —Marilla R. Washburn Bailey,
                    age thirteen in 1852

That first winter, home was still an elusive dream for the newcomers. Home was a temporary place. For some, it was their wagon, if they were lucky enough still to have one. Some moved in with friends or relatives. Hastily-built cabins, shacks, sheds, tents, lean-tos, even trunks of huge trees offered shelter from the constant rains.

> **We may now call ourselves through, they say; and here we are in Oregon making our camp in an ugly bottom, with no home, except our wagons and tent, it is drizzling and the weather looks dark and gloomy.**
> —Amelia Stewart Knight, 1853

Amelia Stewart Knight, her husband and their seven children had arrived from Iowa, leaving most of their treasures and oxen on the trail. The brave band traveled the last part of the journey around Mount Hood over the Barlow Road. It was "14 miles over the worst road that was ever made up and down very steep rough and rocky hills, through mud holes, twisting and winding round stumps, logs, and fallen trees."

After a few days, the family was "all ready for a start again, for some place we dont know where." That some place turned out to be across the Columbia River in the new territory of Washington near Fort Vancouver, where the family moved into "a small log cabin and a lean-to with no windows." The family had traveled the last three days of their long journey shortly after the birth of Amelia's eighth child.

The Stewart sisters—Elizabeth, pregnant with her first child, Mary and Agnes—made their way into the promised land only with the help of rescuers after their wagon train was lost in the Cascade Mountains. Their party of more than 1,000 people

Laurel Hill, Barlow Road

had followed Elijah Elliott, who, it turned out, had never been through that stretch of country. Out of provisions, their cattle worn out, the wagons battered, the beleaguered family was rescued and taken in by settlers near what is now Eugene.

Elizabeth Dixon Smith, ill from constant rain and cold, floated the Columbia River and portaged around the Cascade rapids with her sick husband and their eight children, the youngest a year old. Arriving in the settlement of Portland in late November 1847, Elizabeth "found a small leeky concern with 2 families already in it. You could have stirred us with a stick." Her husband died there six weeks later.

Elizabeth and her children lived in the shed all winter before moving to a place along the Willamette River south of Portland. There she married a widower with ten children a year and a half later. She died six years later at the age of forty-seven.

After the birth of Keturah Belknap's baby in present-day eastern Oregon, mother and child rested a day, then resumed their journey, mother and babe "quite comfortable" on a feather bed in the wagon. From The Dalles, the men took the stock over the Barlow Road. The women and children floated the Columbia in Indian canoes, along with the wagon beds and household goods.

It was late October 1848. The Belknaps settled near the present town of Corvallis, where other friends and family had taken up claims the year before. They were able to build log houses for shelter that first winter, and the area would become known as the "Belknap Settlement."

The woman has survived the journey. She tries not to look back, counting her losses. She looks around her, filling the void with what she has left— family, perhaps new friends, a few treasures from the past—to begin her new life, build her new home. She is among the lucky if she has a trunk full of reminders of home to unpack.

She runs a weather-hardened hand over the battered box and gently opens the lid. The treasures inside are like invisible threads connecting her with home.

The gay colored quilts which came across in a big chest, and which had been used as wrapping for a few cherished dishes and other treasures, were unpacked. . . . Other bits from the old home three thousand miles away were placed on the crude shelves: a picture of grandmother's parents, a few books, the family Bible, the little treasures which had slipped between the bedding in an old chest and queer looking trunk lined with bright flowered paper. They were now at home.[2]

Come you Alsea girls and listen to my noise,
Don't you marry the Oregon boys,
For if you do your fortune it'll be
Cold johnnycakes and venison is all you'll see.

They'll take you to a side-hewed wall
Without any windows in it at all.
Sandstone chimney and a button door,
A clapboard roof and a puncheon
**   floor.**[3]

She slumps down on the hand-hewn bed, gathers the color-laden quilt to her breast and closes her eyes tight, pulling in the warmth and the memory of friends, family and home left behind.

After a time, she opens her eyes, still clutching the cloth of warmth and memory. She looks around her. Thin boards placed loosely over the mud form a dirty, bony floor. A rag dipped in a tin cup filled with elk tallow gives a low light. A thin deer skin flaps over the hole in the wall where a window should be. The string-latch door bounces against the wet wind. Dull light shines through cracks between the logs where they haven't been "chunked" yet.

She becomes aware of the waking up sounds of her baby in the box in the corner. She thinks, *tomorrow I must gather some fern and mix it with mud and fill in those cracks. That will keep out the wind and mice and rats.*

The odor of boiling fish escapes from the pot suspended from an iron bar over the fireplace.

All around her is dull brown. *There's no color here.* She rises, quilt still in hand, and lifts up the deer skin covering the window. All she can see are rain-drenched trees through the dull light. She lets go of the deer skin, then stretches the quilt over it and tucks the top of the quilt into the crack over the deerskin-covered hole.

There. Now there's some color. Next, I can braid a rug from those rags my neighbor brought me. And the gunny bags left from our journey will make curtains and a new table cloth. I'll trim the curtains in red yarn and put them over the window husband promised to put up soon.

After traveling those thousands of miles in their portable canvas homes, those women must have been grateful for some place—any place—to call home. Crude as it was, it gave them some shelter and protection—protection from rain and wind, from animals so bold they sometimes came right up to the door (wolves, sometimes cougars and bears), from increasingly-hostile Indians, and from white marauders who would come and steal whatever they thought they could get away with.

Some of the women had overcome their revulsion toward guns and learned to use them on the trail or soon after their arrival. Marilla Washburn Bailey shot bears, deer, grouse, and pheasants and "became so expert with a revolver that at 50 to 100 feet I could beat most men."[4]

As the women looked around them and scrounged for food to feed their families and tried to keep them safe, I wonder how often they thought to themselves: I came all that distance, went through all that dust and dirt and mud and sickness—*for this*?

Some women were just beginning to make their crude dwelling a home when the monster struck again: the Some Place Else monster.

That Some Place Else monster lured Husband to a place that looked better, or to the gold mines of eastern Oregon, Montana, or Idaho as they opened up. In 1849 and 1850, it was California Gold.

"It was as if some woman-hating shaman had shaken his rattle over Oregon," wrote author

Shannon Applegate. "His incantation was simple enough and but four letters long. Even so, women and children watched helplessly as husbands and fathers vanished before their very eyes. G-O-L-D preempted any consideration of those at H-O-M-E."[5]

—*Skookum* by Shannon Applegate

In her eighties, Keturah Belknap remembered how her family had just gotten settled when

> **Evry thing is excitement the**
> **Calafornie Mines is all the talk, all the**
> **Able Bodyed men are planing to be off**
> **to the mines the familys will double up**
> **and leave one old feable man or a boy**
> **to look after evry two familys. . . . so**
> **we women foalks must try to Hold the**
> **fort, two familys in evry house . . .**[6]

An estimated two out of three of all the able-bodied men in Oregon left for the gold mines. After bringing their mostly-reluctant women across that God-forsaken land, to a place with no home, no plowed field, no crops, the men left.

> **John went to pan for gold**
> **And soon forgot the kids and me**
> —"Overland '52"

Some of the men died of disease, for those were terrible malaria and cholera years. Most came back home. A few struck it rich. Most came back no richer than when they started, and a lot sicker.

After eight months, the Belknap men returned, bringing back "ague" and little gold.

Keturah and George Belknap settled down and helped build their community, especially Keturah's beloved church. After more than twenty-five years, they picked up and moved, first south, then north to Washington, then back again to Oregon, where Keturah lived into her nineties and left five surviving children.

Few newcomers to Oregon stayed where they landed. According to Lillian Schlissel, two out of three settlers had moved again within ten years of their arrival. Hankering for Some Place Else had indeed become a habit for those who had kept moving westward until they'd gone as far west as they could go. Then they simply moved in another direction.

Helen Stewart (Love)'s husband followed the Gold Shaman to eastern Oregon. In their first dozen years in Oregon Country, the family moved seven times.

By her fourteenth wedding anniversary, Elizabeth Paschal Gay and her husband had made twenty-one moves. "My husband was considered a visionary by his friends," she recalled.

Women learned to settle in as fast as they could because they didn't know how long they'd be there.

That first winter, the families survived on whatever food they could get: salmon and potatoes, boiled wheat and peas, milk, butter and deer meat, coffee from dried wheat, barley or peas, ground in coffee mills.

Sunday became a traditional visiting day, and a woman would have to guess how many places to set for the Sunday meal, not knowing who might come visiting.

Sunday Baked Beans[7]
Soak beans over Friday night and boil them on Saturday morning until when you take some in a spoon and

**blow on them the shells split. Then put
them into the big pot in layers with salt
pork. Pour molasses all over it and bake
the rest of Saturday and until noon
Sunday.**

Some pioneer women were not thrilled about
having company to cook for. "Mr B is agoing to
have his house raised and I have got to get diner
for about twenty persons besides being bothered
with two lady visitors," wrote America Rollins
Butler in the Rogue River Valley in 1853. Later, she
wrote that "dinner is over and I am hartly glad of it
for I never did like to cook."

Spring was time for planting "his 'n' her" garden
plots. Precious seeds from home or from new
neighbors were lovingly placed in the soil to bring
forth flowers, leafy vegetables, tomatoes or
"cowcumbers."

She paces out a small plot of ground and marks
it. *This garden plot is mine. In it, I will plant these
seeds my mama gave me when I left home. In the
summer, they'll burst through the wet ground, and
there will be part of home, part of what I left
behind, blooming right here where I planted my
seeds.*

Seeds were so precious to pioneer women that
they would do outlandish things to save them.
Consider the old tale of Dominic, the rooster.[8] It
seems that he made it all the way to Oregon in his
cage piggybacked on the wagon frame, only to
tempt fate in the garden patch. One day the
following spring, he helped himself to the
"cowcumber" seeds ready to be planted.

The seeds' owner, determined to retrieve her
precious treasures, sent her daughters after the
thieving rooster. While the girls held down the

squawking fowl, the mother took her husband's
razor, slit open Dominic's craw, dug out the seeds
and sewed him up with needle and thread. We're
told old Dominic lived a long and happy life—
away from the cucumber patch.

Ma's garden would bring forth vegetables to feed
her family, and herbs to flavor the food and heal
some of the sicknesses that seemed to have
followed her family to their new home, and some
she hadn't heard of.

The women ministered to other families and
cared for each other at the time of birth. Midwives,
or "grannies," were the first healers on the frontier,
as they had been on the trail and back home on
the farm. From oral tradition and practice, they
knew which herbs to grow, how to make them into
remedies, which spices and vegetables make good
poultices.

Poultice for a Stomach Ache[9]
Mix four parts of flour to one of
mustard. Stir in sufficient water to
make a paste. It might burn, but it gets
results.

Midwives knew the lore of limiting the number of
children—knowledge many frontier women desperately sought, weary from a two-decade cycle of
childbearing every two and a half years. To begin
the overland journey with a babe in arms and one

barely weaned, then to discover a pregnancy just as you are trying to build a new home in a strange and threatening place, with no women friends close by—it was almost too much to bear.

Yet the babies kept coming. Many women had little access to midwives or knowledge of birth control methods. Midwives' birth control and abortion concoctions of pantry items like salt, eggs, boric acid and various herbs had little effect. Medical abortions, feasible to urban women, were hardly an option on the frontier.

Isolation from other women was a burden and a danger, especially at the time of birth. Some women received needed care from their husbands. Others didn't get the same consideration routinely given livestock.

> **The week Rhoda was born I cooked**
> **for 15 men who had come to help stack**
> **hay. And in the intervals of serving**
> **them I would creep into my bedroom to**
> **sink across the bed. I was so tired.**
> **Through the bedroom window I could**
> **see the mare and the cow turned out to**
> **pasture for weeks because they were**
> **going to have their young.[10]**
> —Amie Greenwood, Idaho farm wife

For pioneer women, chores in the new home must have seemed like "deja vu all over again." The work was a lot like it had been back on the farm, with added dangers and fewer friends and family to rely on for help and support.

> **It's sweeping at six and**
> **it's dusting at seven,**
> **It's victuals at eight and**
> **it's dishes at nine.**
> **It's potting and panning**

from ten to eleven,
We scarce break our fast
till we plan how to dine.
—"Housewife's Lament"

America Rollins Butler described herself as "maid
of all traids sweeping dusting churning ironing
baking bread and pies dishwashing &c." Like her
sisters on the farm and on the frontier everywhere,
she hated wash day most of all: "Oh! horrors how
shall I express it; is the dreded washing day."

Maybe the worst part of wash day was doing it
alone, facing all that work and no one to share it or
lighten the load. No sounds but the rain and wind
and cries of children when Husband is out in the
field or panning for gold or hunting or gone to
town for supplies. No music except for what you
create yourself.

As I listen to one of my favorite classical tapes, I
realize that most of these women never would hear
the soul-filling sounds of an orchestra. Nor would
they ever have the sounds of music to accompany
their work, as I do.

The journey may have eased the distance
between the woman and her husband as they
moved westward, especially as it got harder and all
they'd had was each other and surviving. Now all
they knew was to try to arrange their lives the way
they had been back home, but this wasn't like
home. Mother may be thousands of miles away.
The closest neighbor might be miles away in this
country where a couple might claim 320 or even
640 acres. That's a lot of distance between
neighbors.

Married women could claim half that land in
their own name under the Donation Land Act, but
there were strings attached. They had to marry in
the right year, and marry a man who had lived in
Oregon long enough to claim the land.

On the frontier, women and men were legally and culturally separated as before. Women took seriously their domestic role, but the frontier was a fragile place. Family breakup, death from accident or violence, divorce, orphaned children, insanity—all were much more likely on the frontier, as Lillian Schlissel illustrated in her story of the Malick family in *Far From Home*.

Those who carved a home in a place fraught with danger as well as opportunity recognized the necessity of community. Women's need for each other's help and companionship was a matter of psychic, if not physical, survival. So they reached out to each other and shared resources.

Sarah Damron Owens told of her joy at an unexpected and precious gift:

> **I had no yarn to knit, nothing to sew, not even scraps or rags to make patches. . . . One of my greatest needs was a cloth for a dish rag. One day Mrs Parrish gave me a sack half full of rags! I am sure I never received a present, before or since, that I so highly appreciated as I did those rags![11]**

Needles were so precious that they were passed around from woman to woman and carefully guarded. The tale of Grandmother Drain's needle became part of Oregon lore.[12]

In her far-flung community at the foot of the Cascades, Grandmother Drain had the only needle. Each woman in the settlement would use it for a few days to mend and patch and quilt, and then she'd pass it on to her nearest neighbor, who might be several miles away.

One day a boy was to deliver the needle back to Mrs. Drain. His mother had poked it in a potato with a bright thread running through the needle's eye for safe keeping. The boy, in his haste to hide from a mother bear he encountered on the way, dropped the potato with the precious needle in it and lost it.

A search party went out. The needle was found and delivered to its owner.

But that's not the end of the story.

Inevitably, the needle broke and the women were getting behind on their sewing until one day a peddler came to town. When he heard the story of the needle and how the boy almost lost it, he reached in his pocket and gave the boy a whole package of needles—enough to deliver one to each woman in the community.

And the peddler? Already savvy in community relations, Aaron Meier would go on to co-found the department store Meier and Frank in Portland.

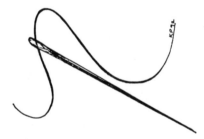

Women used their needles and their skills to fill needs of a growing settlement while filling their apron pockets with extra money.

At the end of her harrowing journey across the plains, sixty-six-year-old Tabitha Brown started a glove-making business with a coin she found in her glove. She used the money to co-found an orphanage in the growing settlement of Forest Grove, planting the seeds that eventually grew to Pacific University.

Harriet Elizabeth Tuctness Bailey, who celebrated her fourth birthday on the trail in 1853, remembered processing and spinning wool as a girl and selling knitted socks for fifty cents a pair. Socks were also legal tender, she recalled. "The merchants used to ship bales of them up into eastern Oregon and into Idaho."[13]

With seeds from home, Sarah Damron Owens in 1844 grew the first flax in her settlement at the mouth of the Columbia. From the crop, she spun twine which she traded with Indians for their fish nets, made fabric for shirts she sold to fishermen, and fashioned a robe for an Indian chief. She did "quite a profitable business in flax," and used the money for shoes, clothing, and food for her growing family.

When her husband bought a band of "Spanish cattle," Sarah Owens noted that a woman "had never attempted to milk one of these vicious animals till I tried it, while my husband stood by with a club."[14]

Sarah Damron Owens trudged across 2,000 miles, grew her own flax crop and fashioned money-making twine and fabric for her family's needs. She milked "vicious animals" and stood guard "with rifle and shot gun" against possible Indian attack.

Imagine trying to be pious and dependent under these circumstances. The woman she had become clashed with what women were still expected to be. Some women used the power they discovered on the trail or from their mothers who had been there to change laws and conditions they no longer could tolerate.

Some even found the courage to be outrageous.

Abigail Jane Scott Duniway, the teenager who lost her mother and her little brother on the trail, would fight for women's right to vote in Oregon and the Northwest for forty-two years until she won. Bethenia Owens-Adair, daughter of Sarah Damron Owens, was three when her family came on the trail. She would marry at fifteen, divorce her abusive husband at nineteen, and become one of

Oregon's first women doctors and an advocate for health care reform.

The longing for beauty and "civilization" remained strong. Both Abigail Scott Duniway and Bethenia Owens-Adair earned money running hat shops for a time.

Many women who couldn't afford a hat still found ways to brighten their world. Elizabeth Gedney wrote of one community where "No matter how ordinary her clothes or how rough her task, nearly every woman wore her bit of ribbon" at the throat of her dress.

I remember how on the trail, Parthenia Blank mourned the loss of a dress when the oxen ate it. Dress-eating bovines were a problem on the frontier too. Marianne Hunsaker Edwards D'Arcy told how the family cow came along and ate a freshly-washed frock hanging out to dry, after her mother had worked months to earn the money to buy fabric for the special dress.

> **Oh Oregon girls, wet Oregon girls,**
> **With laughing eyes and soggy curls;**
> **They'll sing and dance both night and**
> **   day**
> **Til some webfooter comes their way**
> > —parody of "Beulah Land"

Gather 'round the quilt frame and sew the layers together! Invite the men for a Saturday all-night party after the quilting! Put on your best calico and swing your partner!

If you're lucky, you may be invited to a ball.

> **The ball is at last over I am at home**
> **once more O! what an assemblage of**
> **beauty and soft nothings the Ball was**
> **well attended all the youth and beauty**
> **of Jacksonville and the surrounding**

country were present Our supper was splendid . . .
—America Rollins Butler, 1853

The woman lays down her pen, closes her journal, blows out the candle flame. The light of the full moon shines on her through the window—a gift Husband brought from town last week. The shiny new window replaced the deer skin that had covered the hole in the cabin wall.

She gazes out her new window at the field of tall wheat dancing in slow rhythm, caught in the wisps of wind.

She rises, pulls back the quilt and settles in beside her sleeping husband.

She closes her eyes. As she drifts into sleep, she dances back in dreams thousands of miles to the east. . . . Past steep mountains and dusty plains. . . . Past the place where the Indians brought salmon and berries when there was nothing to eat and nothing to give them in return. . . . Past the place on the hill where she and Husband buried their smallest child. . . . Past the Parting of the Ways where she last saw her sister. . . . Past the place where she danced on the green grass.

Ma rocks gently in her old chair with her needlework, humming along softly as Pa strokes his fiddle.

Friends gather around the quilt frame, murmuring secrets and lore.

The child giggles as she chases a butterfly across a flower-carpeted field.

The voices from home and trail remain, somewhere in the corner of a dream or a memory. They will never leave, as long as there are dreams and memory, music and dancing, and hope.

POSTLUDE

Back home, Ruth and I sip coffee in my kitchen, so cozy to me now. I'm reading to her the parts about the housework and the "dreded washing day." She remembers her mother, my Grandma Mae, doing the wash by hand, heating the water on a coal stove, scrubbing the clothes on a washboard, wringing them by hand and lugging them to the clothesline to hang to dry.

"After I was married, Mother used to bring her washing to my house in town and we'd do it together," Ruth remembers. "My parents didn't have electricity where they lived in the country at the time, so Daddy would bring Mother and the wash to my house on Sunday evening. She'd spend the night and the next morning we'd do the wash together.

"After we had the clothes all hung out on the line we'd have lunch and Mother would read our fortunes in the tea leaves."

My mother smiles. "Doing the wash together that way, we actually enjoyed it."

Yes. I know about facing a formidable task and knowing you're not alone. I think back to my first doubts about writing this book, and all the people who helped make it happen—not only family and friends, but people I didn't even know.

Strangers gave me books they thought would be helpful. A museum curator shared a treasure: an Oregon Trail diary someone had just brought to him. I remember the quail hunter who offered us beer. My husband brought me hot late-night meals, listened to my Oregon Trail stories and showered me with hugs and laughs when I needed them. Mother, back home in Colorado, sent me inspiration and helped me figure out which stories to tell. Authors I knew only by their names on books readily gave me their time and advice.

I remember reading one author's prose admiring the pioneer man who cleared the land, erected his own buildings and planted his farm for his family "with his own bare hands and with no help."

I doubt that he did it alone.

While on the trail and at journey's end in a tough and fragile place, the ones most vulnerable were the individuals and families who tried to do it alone. Catherine Thomas Morris, who crossed the plains as a child in 1851, remembered how people helped each other.[1] If a woman got sick, her neighbors came in, "did the housework, took her children to their homes to care for till she was well, brought her home-made bread and jellies and other things," and if a man got sick or had an accident, the men would come and do his work for him.

Men risked their lives to rescue stranded strangers. Women risked their health and that of their families to take in sick and homeless strangers from the trail's end. Families adopted children left orphans from trail tragedies.

As I reflect on the end of my journey, this book, I remember when my older son was still in high school, and he went away for a year to live in another country. As I watched him descend the ramp for the plane that would take him thousands of miles away among strangers, I wanted to call him back and tell him, "You can't leave yet. I haven't told you all you need to know."

As I reach the end of my book I'm thinking: *wait, there's so much I haven't said, so many voices to be heard.*

But just as it was time to let my son go, it's time to let go of this book and the women whose voices fill its pages. I still hear their voices, reminding us to persist in whatever journey we have undertaken.

As we approach a new century, we find we have no more frontiers to settle. Perhaps the women's voices would tell us to persist in building home and community, where we are. But, as the women on the trail discovered, women can't do it alone. And neither can men.

The new frontier is one the women moving westward couldn't imagine: women and men working together as equals to build home and community in a world where masses of people still have no home, still seek a better Some Place Else.

At the opening of the National Historic Oregon Trail Interpretive Center in Baker City, Oregon, Senator Mark Hatfield recalled words of the poet T.S. Eliot as perhaps the most powerful lesson we can learn from the trail that led to the Promised Land:

> **We shall not cease from exploration**
> **And the end of all our exploring**
> **Will be to arrive where we started**
> **And know the place for the first time.**

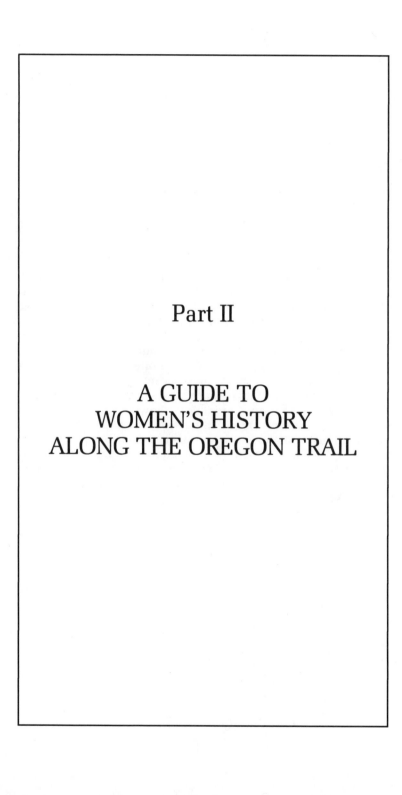

Part II

A GUIDE TO
WOMEN'S HISTORY
ALONG THE OREGON TRAIL

NOTE: The 1993 Oregon Trail 150th Anniversary Celebration has inspired events, festivals, wagon trains, publications, living history, renovation of historic sites and new interpretive centers all along the six-state route. I have listed information resources throughout this section, but please note that circumstances change so I can't guarantee that all information will be current, but it's as close as anyone can get!

The National Park Service offers a comprehensive full-color Oregon Trail map and brochure, showing Trail routes in relation to current major highways, with locations and explanations of major sites, and agency and tourism division contacts. The map/brochure is available at major facilities along the trail, or write to: Oregon National Historic Trail, National Park Service, Pacific Northwest Region, 909 1st Ave., Seattle, WA 98101.

A Guide to Women's History Along the Oregon Trail

> **You can't pass a park without seeing**
> **a statue of some old codger on a horse.**
> **It must be his bravery; you can tell it**
> **isn't his horsemanship. Women are**
> **twice as brave as men, yet they never**
> **seem to have reached the statue stage.**
> —Will Rogers

Oklahoma humorist Will Rogers was right. In any town square in this country, you're much more likely to see a statue of some guy on a horse than one of a woman. But look around. The women are there. You just have to look a little harder. Most won't be on horses. Many of them, like the ubiquitous Pioneer Woman, represent groups of women rather than individual women deemed worthy of remembering.

Come along the Oregon Trail—in your car or your armchair—and find the women. You'll find places along the trail—markers, signposts, landmarks, and historical sites that leave traces of women's presence. Some of these places relate to the Oregon Trail, while others tell of women involved in westering and pioneering both before and after the Oregon Trail era. These women were community builders, story tellers, story makers. Some were outlaws. Some were healers. Some became famous only after they were dead.

This guide isn't intended to take the place of other Oregon Trail guides—books like Gregory

Franzwa's *The Oregon Trail Revisited* and *Maps of the Oregon Trail,* or Aubrey L. Haines' *Historic Sites Along the Oregon Trail.* Use this section to supplement other guides, adding women's presence to enrich the story.

Remember that there was no one Oregon Trail. People bound for Oregon went in the same general direction, but they often fanned out or took cutoffs. For about half the distance, the Oregon Trail merged with or paralleled others—the California Trail and the Mormon (Council Bluffs) Road.

This guide roughly follows the "official" Oregon Trail, designated by Congress in 1978, and identified by the National Park Service. Like the trails, our journey will intersect and mix with other trails, but the main focus is on the official Oregon Trail route.

You'll note that sometimes we'll detour. If some important landmark misses the trail by thirty miles or so, we'll go out of our way to pick it up.

Names of places printed in **plain bold typeface** are Oregon Trail-related. Names of places printed in ***bold italics*** are not trail-related.

So. Let's get started. It's a long journey even in a car or an armchair.

For those traveling the Oregon Trail, I recommend and deeply appreciate the generous support of:

Shilo Inns, with 15 locations for "Affordable Excellence" along the Oregon Trail route: Casper, Wyoming; Idaho Falls; Boise, Idaho (four inns); The Dalles, Oregon; and Portland-Vancouver (eight inns). 11600 SW Barnes Road, Portland, OR 97225. (800) 222-2244.

Best Western Sunridge Inn. Free shuttle service to the National Historic Oregon Trail Interpretive Center. One Sunridge Lane, Baker City, OR 97814. (800) 233-2368.

MISSOURI

Oregon Trail emigrants' hardships didn't start at Independence, the official "jumping-off" place in the early years. Many traveled the dangerous waters of the Missouri River to Independence, while others made the cold and arduous journey by wagon.

As more northern routes opened to the Platte River Road, jumping-off places shifted northward to St. Joseph and Omaha. Independence remains the official beginning of the Oregon Trail today.

INDEPENDENCE

(1) The National Frontier Trails Center (318 West Pacific)

As described in Chapter I, the National Frontier Trails Center's displays take you along each of the westward trails—to Santa Fe, Salt Lake, California, and Oregon. Diary excerpts from the people who traveled the trail narrate the journey. Women and children are well-represented.

Photographs, paintings, artifacts, an introductory movie and audio recordings enhance your journey. If you want to do some research on the Oregon Trail or find out about the Oregon-California Trails Association, this is the place.

Open weekdays 9-4:30, Sat-Sun 12:30-4:30. Admission charge. (816) 254-0059.

Also in the National Frontier Trails Center are:

The Pioneer Woman Statue

Although this is not officially Oregon Trail related, the bronze statue of the young mother in the courtyard holding her child and gazing westward captures the spirit of the women who pioneered the ever-expanding West. Internationally-known sculptor Juan Lombardo crafted this poignant statue, "honoring the women who built this nation."

Accompanying the statue is a commemorative album with photographs and commentary honoring twenty women who shaped the history of Independence, including First Lady Bess Wallace Truman and black businesswoman Emily Fisher.

Contemporary Album Quilt

This colorful quilt, fashioned after popular nineteenth-century album quilts, represents the work of members of community organizations, who made individual blocks and pieced them together. Like early album quilts, this one's makers signed their blocks.

Women leaving on the long westward journey often received album or friendship quilts from their friends as a parting gift to warm their hearts and bodies during their trek.

(2) Independence Courthouse Square (Lexington and Liberty Streets)

Independence was a raucous, noisy place, its muddy streets lined with merchants' shops, cheap hotels and grog shops, and filled with seasoned trappers and neophyte gunslingers sporting their new purchases. Spread out for miles were the tents of emigrant campers waiting to begin the journey.

According to Bill Bullard, Administrator of the National Frontier Trails Center, emigrants really did gather in one place to begin the westward journey—sort of like an official starting point for a race. To hear Bullard describe it,

the take-off must have been something like a Keystone
Kops routine because of inexperienced ox drivers trying to
figure out how to maneuver the animals. In fact, Bullard
says, it was so slow that the lead wagon often would be
ready to camp before the last one on the train would be
ready to roll. Fortunately, they got better with practice.

The stately courthouse in the square isn't the one that
was there when the emigrants left, but you can find a
monument marking the beginning of the Oregon and Santa
Fe Trails, which followed the same route until they parted
near the town of Gardner, Kansas, southwest of Kansas City.

KANSAS CITY
(3) Pioneer Mother Statue (Penn Valley Park, Pershing Road
and Main)

This statue depicts a determined young mother riding a
horse with a babe snuggled in her lap. Accompanying her
on foot is a grizzled-looking man with a rifle slung over his
shoulder. The statue bears an inscription from the book of
Ruth, familiar to many an Oregon Trail traveler: "Where
thou goest I will go, Where thou lodgest I will lodge."

(4) Children's Mercy Hospital (2401 Gillham Road)

Two widowed sisters, Dr. Alice Berry Graham (a dentist)
and Dr. Katharine Berry Richardson (a surgeon), founded
this facility in 1897 to provide free care for needy children.
After her sister's death, Dr. Richardson continued to keep
the hospital going. Dr. Richardson relaxed by working with
carpenters in the basement of the nurses' home rebuilding
furniture for the nurses. A plaque honors the two sisters
inside today's modern facility, which continues the pioneer
doctors' policy of free care.

(5) Women's Leadership Fountain (9th and Paseo)

The oldest working fountain in Kansas City has been
refurbished and now honors forty-four Kansas City women
history makers, including Drs. Graham and Richardson.
Fifteen leading local women's organizations sponsored the
project and maintain the fountain.

KANSAS

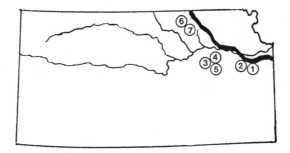

Kansas honors its Oregon Trail heritage with living history at historical sites, tours of the trail, wagon treks, festivals like Bullwhacker Days, and dramatizations at Oregon Trail sites. For information, contact the Kansas Division of Travel & Tourism, 400 SW 8th St. #500, Topeka, KS 66603. (913) 296-2009.

Several theories explain the origin of the name "Kansas." One attributes the name to the Indians who lived on the prairies and called themselves the "wind people."

On Kansas roads and highways, watch for small triangular white and red Oregon Trail National Historic Trail signs. They mark known trail crossings. The emigrants saw mostly grass and wildflowers across the rolling prairies of present-day Kansas. Pioneers who claimed the land after the emigrants made their way west planted many of the trees seen there today. The trees reminded them of home.

LAWRENCE

(1) Lucy Hobbs Taylor Building (809 Vermont)

In case you pass this building, you'll know that it's named for the American woman who pioneered in dentistry. Lucy Hobbs Taylor courageously pursued her education despite extreme prejudice and harassment, becoming in 1866 the first American woman to earn her dental degree.

(2) Museum of Anthropology (Jayhawk Boulevard, University of Kansas)

Located in Spooner Hall, this museum's collection of worldwide ethnic objects includes Plains Indians beadwork.

TOPEKA

Interstate 70 to Topeka is right on top of what was the Oregon Trail, which went through present-day downtown Topeka. In Topeka, you can see:

(3) *Pioneer Woman Statue* (State House grounds)

Suffragist, magazine editor, and publisher Lilla Day Monroe became the first woman admitted to practice before the Kansas Supreme Court in 1895. She spearheaded the drive to erect this striking bronze statue of a mother poised with a rifle over her knee protecting her children. (Most pioneer mothers did not pack a rifle although some did, in fact, use one to protect home and family from Indians and white marauders.)

Lilla Day Monroe collected more than 800 Kansas pioneer women's accounts, published decades later by her great-granddaughter, Joanna Stratton, in her 1981 book, *Pioneer Women: Voices from the Kansas Frontier*.

(4) Ward-Meade Park (124 N. Fillmore)

Mary Jane Ward, who called herself the "Mother of Topeka," burned a candle to guide weary Oregon Trail travelers to the doors of her cabin, one of Topeka's first, built in 1854. A candle in the window still greets visitors to the reconstructed Ward Cabin, part of a living history community on the park grounds. Here, a present-day Mary Jane Ward may serve you a hearthside meal, topped off with her special ash cakes.

Mary Jane Ward's Ash Cakes
(recipe courtesy of Ward-Meade Home)
After the children were in bed, the adults often gathered around the hearth to enjoy Mary Jane's special cakes:
Prepare a stiff dough of 1 quart corn meal, sifted, 1 teaspoon salt and some water. Knead well. Pat the cakes into shape by throwing them quickly from one hand to the other, back and forth again and again until achieving the desired rounded or oval shape.
Sweep a clean place in the hottest part of the hearth. Wrap each cake in green cabbage leaves or corn husks. Cover with hot ashes. When done, rake out the cakes, wipe clean. They should be eaten immediately with butter, if you have it.

Ward-Meade Park is open year-round Tues-Fri 10-4, plus Sat-Sun 1-4 in summer. Admission charge. (913) 235-0806.

(5) Kansas Museum of History (6425 SW 6th Street)

This complex is a gold mine of women's and Oregon Trail history, with displays depicting women's roles in missionary work, trails through Kansas, and pioneering. Also featured is women's extensive involvement in reform movements, including woman suffrage and the Populist movement, led by Mary ("raise less corn and more hell") Lease.

Here, you can also see some of Carry Nation's weapons— a hammer and a club—used in her eleven-year war against liquor, beginning in 1900. A mirror fragment saved from her famous attack on the Senate Saloon offers evidence of the six-foot temperance leader's ability to wreck a bar in seconds. One judge who sent her to jail muttered, "God forgive me for not strangling her with my bare hands."

Regarded as a self-righteous fanatic, Carry Nation was one of many women whose anger came from witnessing the family destruction caused by alcoholism.

The museum is open year-round except for major holidays Mon-Sat 9-4:30, Sun 12:30-4:30. (913) 272-8681.

From Topeka to the Nebraska border, the trail heads northwest, crossing and paralleling various highway routes. Watch for Oregon Trail markers and crossing signs. Fields are mostly cultivated, but now and then you think you can see the wagon tracks. Are they really there or are they just teasing your imagination?

BLUE RAPIDS

(6) Alcove Spring information panel (junction of US 77 and Kansas 9)

The spring itself is on private land, six miles northwest of the marker. Oregon Trail travelers named the spring in 1846, calling the cascade of water above it "beautiful" and "romantic." Just north of Alcove Spring was Independence Crossing, where emigrants forded the Big Blue River.

The information panel beside a pleasant picnic area mentions explorer John Charles Fremont's passage through here in 1842, and that of Marcus Whitman, leading the 1843 Great Migration to Oregon. The Reverend Whitman had established a mission in 1836, with his wife, Narcissa, in present-day southeastern Washington. Narcissa Whitman and another missionary, Eliza Spalding, were the first two white women to cross the Rockies to western lands.

The panel notes the death of Sarah Keyes of the ill-fated 1846 Donner Party, near Alcove Spring. Grandma Keyes, seventy years old and gravely ill, insisted on starting west with her family, and had her own rocking chair in a special wagon.

Her granddaughter, Virginia Reed, noted in her diary,

> **We buried her verry decent We made a nete coffin and buried her under a tree we had a head stone and had her name cutonit . . . We miss her verry much evry time we come in the wagon we look up at the bed for her.**

Death at this beautiful spot spared Grandma Keyes the horror her family would later encounter in the bitter Sierra Nevadas. A monument on private land near the spring honors this spirited woman.

(7) *Blue Rapids Public Library* (Blue Rapids town square)

The building that grew from the "Ladies' Library" is testimony to women's community-building on the frontier. Pioneer women met in 1874 and opened the town's first library in a store with 143 books. The library moved into its current home in the then-new building two years later.

NEBRASKA

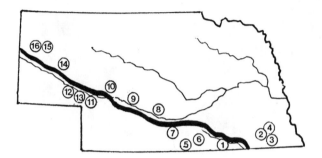

In what is now Nebraska, the travelers followed
the Little Blue River almost to the Platte River, with
a dry stretch in between. The state's name derives
from Indian language for "flat water," encountered
in abundance by travelers, past and present.

For information on Nebraska's Oregon Trail
activities, contact Division of Travel and Tourism,
Department of Economic Development, 301 Centennial Mall South, Lincoln, NE 68509-4666. (800)
426-6505.

FAIRBURY
(1) Rock Creek Station (about six miles southeast of Fairbury)

This was a way-station and toll bridge crossing for
Oregon Trail travelers from the late 1850s and into the '60s,
but that's not what Rock Creek Station became famous for.
Here's where Wild Bill Hickok began his infamous career as
a gunfighter.

Depending on which account you read, Wild Bill was
either a hero or a villain of the gunfight at Rock Creek
Station, and a woman may have held a key to the mystery.
When David McCanles and two companions came to the
station keeper's house to collect some money owed him,
Wild Bill Hickok shot McCanles. Whether Wild Bill was

Rock Creek Station

defending the station keeper's wife from a belligerent McCanles and his "gang," or ending an argument fueled by an angry woman, who's to say?

(Calamity) Jane Cannary (pronounced CANery) defended her one true love, Wild Bill: "[H]e killed a bunch of murderers in self defense becoming famous as a crack shot with either hand."[1]

The current official account portrays Hickok as a trigger-happy varmint who, with his buddies, gunned down three unarmed men.

Today, Rock Creek Station State Historical Park has an interpretive center and facilities for picnics, hiking, and camping. Trail ruts, deepened by erosion, run through the park. The grounds are open year-round. The visitor center is open daily 9-5 in summer, weekends 1-5 spring and fall. Park entry permit required. (402) 729-5777.

BEATRICE
(2) Homestead National Monument (4.5 miles northwest of Beatrice on State 4), National Park Service

A twenty-five-mile detour here from Rock Creek Station is well worth the trip. Here, you get a feel for the relationship of the westward migration and settlement of the "Great American Desert." Congress passed the Homestead Act in 1862—after most of the migration to the west coast had taken place. Only then did most people to

Homestead National Monument

the East regard the lands between the Missouri River and the west coast as a likely place to settle.

Given plenty of time, visitors can follow miles of trails through a restored tall grass prairie and visit a pioneer home and school house, much like the ones the Oregon Trail emigrants built once they settled halfway across the continent. The visitor center is informative, but the slide show we saw was told through men's eyes, and few women were seen or heard.

Daniel Freeman claimed a 160-acre homestead here in 1863. His second wife, Agnes Freeman, although hardly mentioned, is worthy of note. A self-described "cantankerous" woman, she managed to get a state license to practice medicine while raising six children. Monuments mark their grave sites.

Hearing and visually-impaired assistance available. Open daily 8-6 in summer, 8:30-5 in winter. Free admission. (402) 223-3514.

(3) Gage County Historical Museum (2nd and Court Street) and **(4) Chautauqua Park** (US 77 South)

At this museum housed in the old railroad depot, ask the hosts about one of the county's most famous citizens, Clara Colby. A moving force behind establishing the town library and Chautauqua Park, Colby began publishing *The Woman's Tribune* in 1883. The weekly newspaper became the official voice of the national woman suffrage movement. Clara Colby lectured across the US and abroad on many subjects, including world peace.

The museum is open year-round Tues-Sat 9-12 and 1-5, Sun 1:30-5. Donations accepted. (402) 228-1679.

The park (not connected with the museum) offers camping with electric hook-ups, picnicking, showers, and tennis courts.

County roads continue to crisscross the Oregon Trail route as the emigrants followed the Blue River almost to the Platte River road.

RED CLOUD

(5) *Willa Cather Historical Center* (338 North Webster Street)

Another detour from the trail takes the traveler to the home of Willa Cather, one of the most eloquent chroniclers of the mid-western frontier. Born in Virginia, she grew to love the sky-filled grasslands and recorded their moods and stories in such books as *Oh Pioneers!* and *My Antonia.*

"Trees were so rare in that country," Cather wrote, ". . . that we used to feel anxious about them, and visit them as if they were persons."

The Willa Cather museum, operated by the Nebraska State Historical Society, plus an art gallery and book store, are in downtown Red Cloud on North Webster Street. Hours vary according to the time of year. Admission charge. Guided tours of Willa Cather home are available. (402) 746-3285.

Guided tours of the museum are also available, and visitors can take a self-guided tour of the town and countryside, finding places Cather wrote about.

Five and a half miles south of town is what the Pulitzer prize-winning author would have loved the most—the Willa Cather Memorial Prairie, 610 acres of native grasslands preserved by the Nature Conservancy in Willa Cather's honor.

DEWEESE

(6) Spring Ranch (about 6 1/2 miles northwest of Deweese, but ask locals. Roads are confusing.)

This is a quiet place where the visitor can walk among old buildings or see where they used to stand. There are no restaurants or information booths or Chamber of Commerce here, so let your imagination take over and simply enjoy the silence.

Spring Ranch

Spring Ranch was a "road ranch" (pioneer-day motel) stop after the Oregon Trail became a more civilized road in the late 1850s and '60s. Gregory Franzwa's *Maps of the Oregon Trail* shows the grave of Elizabeth Taylor southwest of the ghost town of Spring Ranch. She was the only woman known to have been lynched in Nebraska— apparently for being uppity and prosperous and refusing cattlemen's advances.[2] Elizabeth and her brother were hanged in 1885. Charges against her were later dropped— too late for Elizabeth and her brother.

KENESAW

(7) Susan Hail grave information panel (4 miles northwest of Kenesaw)

This panel is beside the highway, surrounded by farm land. Here is a poignant story of high hopes and dashed dreams. By this point on the trail during peak cholera years, emigrants could almost follow the way by the graves. The disease claimed a thirty-four-year-old bride, Susan O. Hail, in 1852. According to legend, her grieving husband buried her in a coffin made of wagon lumber. Terrified that he wouldn't be able to find the grave again, he temporarily marked the grave and returned to Missouri, where he had a stone marker made. Then he trudged all the way back, pushing a wheelbarrow with the marker for his wife's resting place.

According to author Aubrey L. Haines, the grave itself is .6 miles due east of the panel adjacent to an unimproved farm road. The stone over the grave is not the original one brought by Susan Hail's husband.

KEARNEY
(8) Fort Kearny State Historical Park (3 miles south of I-80, south of Kearney)

The first fort built to protect Oregon Trail travelers, Fort Kearny (pronounced Kar-ney) was built in 1848. It served more as a pony express and stage coach stop, a supply station, and the first point for mailing and receiving precious letters.

Fort personnel also kept records of westward-bound travelers—invaluable for historians. Helen Stewart wrote in 1853:

> **. . . we pass fort carney there was a soldier**
> **came and got the number of all of us and our**
> **cattle and he told us that there was a thirteen**
> **thousand head of people and ninety thousand**
> **head of stock the largest emigration has ever**

**past yet we camp not very good grass no wood
except a few willows it is comeing up another
storm . . .**

Abigail Scott Duniway wrote of Fort Kearny in 1852:

**We here halted awhile to write letters, look
at curiosities, &c. The fort is a rather shabby
looking concern but contains two very good
looking dwelling houses which to us who had
been traveling for three weeks without seeing a
house or any thing like civilization presented
an appearance of a very pleasing nature.**

The site, operated by the Nebraska Game and Parks
Commission, is open year-round. Hours vary. Park permit
required. (308) 234-9513.

The nearby Fort Kearny State Recreation Area has a
campground, picnic shelters, hiking-biking trail, swimming,
canoeing and fishing, including handicap accessible fishing.
Watch for the arrival of sandhill cranes in the spring.
Nebraska State Park Permit required.

NORTH PLATTE

(9) Buffalo Bill Ranch State Historical Park (US 83 to US 30, 2
miles west) Nebraska Game and Parks Commission

Buffalo Bill Cody, who was an assistant wagon master on
a bull train at the age of twelve, provided buffalo meat for
railroad workers in the late 1860s. He is said to have killed
4,280 buffalo in eight months.

In the barn, you'll find mention of sharpshooter and trick
rider Annie Oakley. An important part of Buffalo Bill's Wild
West Shows of the late 1800s, her popularity rivaled that of
Buffalo Bill.[3] As a young girl, Annie could handle a gun so
well that she paid off her widowed mother's mortgage with
the money she made hunting. Contrary to the movie story,
she won the heart of her hero, Frank Butler, by outshooting
him.

Calamity Jane was also a sharpshooter and trick rider for
Buffalo Bill's Wild West Shows, though for a shorter period
of time. She described one of her tricks in a letter to her
daughter: "I ride a horse bare back, standing up, shoot my
old Stetson hat twice after throwing it in the air before it
falls back on my head."[4]

Park hours vary. Park entry permit required. (308)
532-4795.

O'Fallon's Bluff

SUTHERLAND
(10) O'Fallon's Bluff (Eastbound exit I-80, Sutherland Rest
Area)

This is one of the most graphic and accessible areas to
see pristine ruts along the trail. Old wagon wheels mark the
ruts, formed as wagons had to narrow their path to pass
between the bluff and the Platte River.

Author Irene Paden wrote that the stage coach drivers
and stock tenders who traveled the trail in later years used
the huge anthills in the area for free dry cleaning. They
would leave vermin-infested blankets and clothing over the
anthills for the little critters to feast on. I haven't found
references to this practice in emigrant women's diaries. My
husband doubts my theory that it's because the ladies
didn't have problems with lice and fleas.

OGALLALA
(11) Boot Hill (3 blocks west of State 61 & North Spruce)

Before Boot Hill became a final resting place for gun
fighters, horse thieves and other unsavory characters,
respectable people were buried here. Among them was Mrs.
Lillie Miller, a young mother and an early pioneer. She and
her infant died in childbirth. Both were buried in the
cemetery on the hill. When the tough guys took over the
hill, buried with their boots on, the proper inhabitants were
moved to the respectable cemetery.

When workers went to exhume the bodies of Lillie and her baby, they discovered an amazing thing: what was claimed to be the first case of human petrification. Lillie's body had turned to stone, and, according to the local paper, she "appeared almost as she was in life. Even the skin was on the face, and the body showed no signs of putrification or decay." Adding to the puzzle was the fact that all that remained of the child's body was bones. Workers had to use a derrick to remove Lillie's body.

A memorial stone and fenced gravesite remain where Lillie Miller and her baby once rested on Boot Hill.

Lillie Miller grave

LEWELLEN
(12) Ash Hollow State Historical Park (one-half mile east and three miles south of Lewellen off US 26)

The emigrants would have crossed the South Platte near what is now Brule, and traveled along a bluff toward the North Platte. At Windlass Hill, two miles south of Ash Hollow, the men lowered the wagons down from the bluffs onto the valley floor, slowing the wagons with ropes and oxen.

Irene Paden's book *The Wake of the Prairie Schooner* makes an interesting point. It wouldn't have required more than a day's work for a team of men to build a passable road into the hollow, but no one ever did. They couldn't afford the time to build a road or allow anyone else to get ahead of them. "Any captain would rather let the whole emigration fall down Windlass Hill than have that happen," according to Paden's book.

At Ash Hollow, the tired travelers rested, repaired wagons, left mail to be picked up at a trapper's cabin, and drank from the lovely—and deadly—waters of Ash Hollow Spring. In high cholera years, the still water harbored cholera bacteria. The cemetery to the south bears testament to the dangers lurking in the beauty of Ash Hollow.

At the top of a bluff is an interpretive center, near Ash Hollow Cave, used for centuries by Indians and their ancestors. The Nebraska Game and Parks Commission runs the 1,000-acre park. Inquire about a special program about women on the Oregon Trail.

Picnic area. Wheel chair accessible. Open daily Memorial Day-Labor Day 8-6. Park entry permit required. (308) 778-5651.

Ash Hollow Spring

(13) Ash Hollow Cemetery and Rachel Pattison Grave (north of Ash Hollow off US 26)

A glass-enclosed stone monument marks the grave of Rachel Pattison, an eighteen-year-old bride who died of cholera while traveling with her new husband's Oregon-bound family in 1849. Young Rachel was the first to be buried in the cemetery. Her grieving husband, like many other bereaved emigrants, wrote a detailed description of the location of his bride's hastily-prepared grave, in the hope of some day returning to where she lay. He, like most of the others, never came back.

LISCO
(14) Narcissa Whitman Marker (5 1/2 miles west of Lisco on US 26)

The marker commemorates the missionary's 1836 passage through this country.

Narcissa Whitman and Eliza Spalding accompanied their husbands to the Northwest to "civilize" the Indian "savages," and became the first white women to cross the Rockies. Narcissa and her new husband, Marcus, established their mission in present-day southeastern Washington.

In his book *Platte River Road Narratives*, Merrill J. Mattes declared that on the journey west, the missionary ladies "were spared cooking chores for . . . their husbands did all the work." Don't believe it. Read Narcissa Whitman's journals for the true story.

SCOTTSBLUFF
(15) Rebecca Winters marker and grave (3 miles east of downtown Scottsbluff on a pullout off truck route 26)

A marker honors Rebecca Winters, a Mormon emigrant who died of cholera on her way to the Promised Land in 1862 at the age of fifty. Friends and family marked her grave on an iron wagon tire. When railroad surveyors found the crude marker, they plotted the tracks around the grave so it wouldn't be disturbed.

The grave itself, marked with the original tire iron, is about a quarter of a mile west along the tracks.

GERING
Check out Gering's celebration of Oregon Trail Days the third week of July. Scottsbluff/Gering United Chamber of Commerce, PO Box 1350 (HH), Scottsbluff, NE 69363. (308) 632-2133.

(16) Scotts Bluff National Monument (3 miles west of Gering on State 92)

Indians called this magnificent rock formation ME-A-PA-TE ("hill that is hard to go around"). Emigrants called it Scott's Bluffs, after fur trapper Hiram Scott, who died near its base after fellow trappers abandoned the poor fellow.

The National Park Service manages this national monument and the visitor center, which contains a large collection of William Henry Jackson paintings of Oregon Trail scenes. Men's voices dominated the slide show we saw here. One man's words particularly struck me: "How I wish the Indians would attack. I'm so bored."

You can spend a lot of time exploring this place, by foot or by car. On a hot, windy day, I headed west on foot from the visitor center, watching for rattlesnakes, through nearly hip-deep wagon ruts ground into the rock of Mitchell Pass.

Even this far, some travelers had seen enough of the elephant (an emigrant expression for facing hardships on the trail). They'd seen too much sickness and dying, too much dust, and turned back toward home. Walking that lonely, hot, snake-inhabited path, surrounded by ominous-looking rock formations, I could understand why.

The visitor center is open daily 8-6 summer, 8-5 winter, closed federal holidays. Permit required. (308) 436-4340.

Scott's Bluff

WYOMING

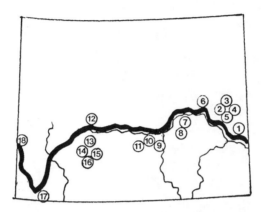

The name Wyoming, transplanted from the East, comes from two Delaware Indian words, MECHEWEAMI-ING, meaning "on the great plain."

Wyoming is called the Equality State for good reason. Wyoming was the first state or territory formally to allow women to vote. The state also claims the first woman Justice of the Peace (Esther Hobart Morris, 1870); first all-woman jury (1870— although a judge later took women off juries and they didn't serve in Wyoming again until 1950); first woman governor (Nellie Tayloe Ross, 1925); first woman to head the US Mint (Nellie Tayloe Ross, 1933); first woman bailiff (Mary Atkinson,1870); first woman statewide elected official (Estelle Reed, 1894).

In Cheyenne, the State Capital, the stately statue of Esther Morris graces the front entrance to the Capitol building. At the Old Governor's Mansion a few blocks away, Nellie Tayloe Ross's photograph is among those of both Wyoming governors and

governors' wives. The state museum, however, gives the impression that after the Indians, the only history in Wyoming is cowboys, loggers, miners, and ladies lounging in their parlors. Amazingly, there's no mention of why Wyoming is the Equality State.

Communities and historic sites throughout Wyoming are actively involved in celebrating their Oregon Trail heritage with new and upgraded interpretive sites, festivals, living history and wagon trains. The Wyoming Division of Tourism and The Wagner Perspective have produced a self-guided tour map and brochure, *Wagons Across Wyoming: Oregon Trail 150 Years*. For information or the brochure, contact the Wyoming Division of Tourism, I-25 at College Drive, Cheyenne, WY 82002 (307) 777-7777.

The trail through what is now Wyoming took the emigrants through the eerie rock formations, alkali water, and dusty roads of the Black Hills; across endless sage prairies; and through the fabled and surprisingly flat South Pass into what was Oregon Country. More graves and animal carcasses and abandoned treasures marked the path.

FORT LARAMIE

A new information center, constructed with volunteer help, is on US 26 in the middle of town.

(1) Fort Laramie (about 3 miles southwest of the town of Fort Laramie, off Route 26)

Fort Laramie, an early trading post, became a military post in 1849. The fort without walls was an important supply post, Laramie River ferry and bridge crossing, and rest stop for the emigrants.

Elizabeth Goltra wrote in 1853: "There are about 300 wagons waiting to cross Laramie River, they tell us we can cross tomorrow evening, we take this opportunity to wash and bake."

Choosing not to wait, Elizabeth's party decided to caulk their wagon and float across the river. They "crossed with safety," she wrote, and "while crossing word came that the ferry boat had sunk with a heavy wagon."

"Old Bedlam," the oldest and most famous building, was the old post headquarters and bachelor housing. In the Civil War period, Catharine Collins, the commander's wife, lived with her husband on the second floor and managed the officers' mess hall.

Fort Laramie

The fort's cooperative relations with Indians degenerated into attacks and broken treaties from the 1850s through the 1870s, when government policies finally pushed the Plains Indians onto reservations. Eight miles east of Fort Laramie is the site of the 1854 Gratton Massacre, a needless tragedy that began over an emigrant's lost cow. Fort Laramie served as the center of the Great Sioux Campaign of 1876, the final Indian attempt to protect their lands and way of life.

Fort Laramie, managed by the National Park Service, has living history demonstrations, interpretive talks and conducted tours in summer. The old Commissary Building houses the visitor center. Open daily 8-4:30, with extended summer hours. Federal Entrance Fee area. (307) 837-2221.

Hog Ranch (west of Fort Laramie)

The book *Wyoming: A Guide to Historic Sites* delicately describes the bar and brothel establishment close to Fort Laramie as "typical of those near military posts, providing billiards, cards, whiskey, and companionship for troops and travelers." A customer speculated on why it was called a hog ranch: "I never saw any hogs around . . . , but think perhaps it had reference to the girls as they were a very low, tough set."

According to another visitor, there was a "nest" of ranches in this area, each "equipped with a rum-mill of the worst kind and each contained from three to half a dozen Cyprians . . . . I have never seen a lower, more beastly set of people of both sexes." The only redeeming feature of the "ranch," according to yet another observer, was that you could get good, cheap meals here.

The name hog ranch follows the historical habit of labeling women as animals: bitch, chick, dove, bird, cow, heifer. (And let's not forget Nevada's famous "Mustang Ranch.") In the case of Hog Ranch, the animal is the lowest and dirtiest one could think of.

Equating prostitutes with "Cyprians" was a negative reference to residents of the Mediterranean island of Cyprus, where women in pre-Christian times celebrated their sexuality in rites to the goddesses Aphrodite and Astarte.

Historians suggest that frontier "soiled doves" were, for the most part, searching for a better life—economic independence, escape from isolated farms and ranches, a better man. They rarely found a better life or a better man.

The remains of this "hog ranch" are not open to the public.

GUERNSEY
(2) Guernsey Roadside Rest Area (US 26 just east of State 270 and the town of Guernsey)

Here, ten unique sighting devices invite the curious to peer through them and locate landmarks including Laramie Peak, the Guernsey Ruts area, and Register Cliff, where emigrants added their names to those of early trappers and traders.

Register Cliff

(3) Register Cliff (2.8 miles southeast of Guernsey)

On this soft sandstone cliff, the "Kilroy-was-here" instinct left names of early trappers, traders and emigrants, along with "Frank, 1957" and "Lisa '89."

(4) Oregon Trail Ruts National Historic Landmark (1.3 miles south of Guernsey and US 26 on a good country road. Follow signs out of Guernsey to a parking area. A short foot trail leads to the ruts.)

Here, emigrants had to narrow their path to cross this sand rock formation. The thousands of wagon wheels cut through the soft stone to form perhaps the starkest, most evocative ruts on the trail. Beside the shoulder-deep ruts you can even see the footpaths worn by bullwhackers walking beside their teams.

Don't miss it!

Guernsey Ruts

(5) Lucinda Rollins Grave (near Oregon Trail Ruts on a hill overlooking the North Platte River)

A white cement monument used to hold the original headstone of Lucinda Rollins' grave until vandals got to it. The twenty-four-year-old Ohio woman died on the trail in 1849.

DOUGLAS

(6) Fort Fetterman sign (west of Douglas off I-25)

Fort Fetterman was an army outpost that served as a base for General Crook's expedition that ended in his defeat in the 1876 Battle of the Rosebud. According to this sign, one of his teamsters was none other than "Calamity" Jane Cannary.

So much myth grew around this raucous woman that it's impossible to separate fact from fiction. She apparently crossed the plains to Montana with her family in 1865 when she was about thirteen. After she was orphaned, she became a drifter. This colorful character often wore men's clothes—the only appropriate garb for the exploits she claimed as a bullwhacker, army scout, railroad worker, stagecoach driver, and Indian fighter. She was also rumored to have stationed herself occasionally at Fort Laramie's "hog ranch."

Calamity Jane gave away most of her money to people she thought needed it more than she did. She employed her skills as a nurse, especially during the 1878 Deadwood smallpox epidemic, and earned money—and appreciation—for her cooking skills.

Calamity Jane's Receipt for 20 Year Cake
(Adapted from *Calamity Jane's Letters* to her Daughter)

Mix together 25 eggs beaten separate, 2 1/2 pounds each of sugar, flour and butter, 7 1/2 pounds seeded raisins, 1 1/2 pounds citron cut very fine, 5 pounds currants, 1/4 ounce cloves, 1/2 ounces cinnamon, 2 ounces mace, 2 ounces nutmeat, 2 teaspoons yeast powder or 2 teaspoons soda & 3 cream tartar. Bake.

This will make 3 cakes 8 pound each. Pour a pint of brandy over the cakes while still warm. Seal in tight crock. This cake is unexcelled & will keep good to the last crum 20 years.

The restored Fort Fetterman State Historic Site, which gained fame in western author Owen Wister's *The Virginian*, is seven miles west of Douglas, off Wyoming 93.

North of Fort Fetterman, according to my map, was the site of another "hog ranch," "the most notorious gambling resort and saloon in the territory." Resort? Interesting description.

CASPER

The Bureau of Land Management plans to open The Wyoming Historic Trail Visitor Center in Casper in 1994.

(7) Fort Caspar Museum (4001 Fort Caspar Road)

The museum has exhibits on American Indian and Euro-American history of the area and a full-size replica of the 1847 Mormon ferry across the North Platte.

The reconstructed fort and interpretive center form the centerpiece of a city of Casper park complex. Open year-round Mon-Fri 9-5, Sun 1-4. Extended hours in summer. (307) 235-8462.

(8) Squaw Creek Road sign (just south of the State 220 turnoff south of Casper)

This is just one of many landmarks and signs referring to squaws, the emigrants' common term for American Indian women. To the emigrants, "Indians" referred only to men. Indian women were merely "squaws."

The term "squaw" reinforced the Indian women's low status in the eyes of both male and female emigrants. It was important to emigrant women to believe that no matter how low they sank, they were still more "civilized" than the Indian women. Hence, the belittling term "squaw."

What they didn't know—and what most people still don't know—is the ancient meaning of the word squaw. Depending on the tribe and the historical era, American Indian women held great power within their tribes. The word "squaw" meant queen or lady. A sunksquaw was a woman chief.

ALCOVA

(9) Alcova Reservoir (southwest of Casper off State 220)

The waters of this reservoir have flooded the place where Ella Watson, alias Cattle Kate, was lynched—the only Wyoming woman known to have suffered that fate. A skilled rancher, she brazenly rode straddle instead of sidesaddle, as ladies were supposed to do. Some say Kate ran another kind of ranch on her homestead—a "hog ranch."

Some say she wasn't married to her ranching partner, Jim Averill. Others say she was, but kept her marriage a secret because a wife could not claim a homestead in her own right. Like Elizabeth Taylor, who was lynched in Nebraska, it appears that Cattle Kate's greatest crime may have been being an uppity woman. Both she and Jim were lynched on that fateful day in 1889.

Cattle Kate's lynching brought an indignant response from a Salt Lake City newspaper:

"The men of Wyoming will not be proud of the fact that a woman—albeit unsexed and totally depraved—has been hanged within their territory," the editor huffed. "That is about the poorest use that a woman can be put to."[1]

(10) INDEPENDENCE ROCK STATE HISTORIC SITE (50 miles southwest of Casper on State 220)

Emigrants could gauge their progress by whether or not they reached this famous landmark by July 4. Many celebrated Independence Day shooting off cannons, dancing and drinking precious whiskey in the shadow of this hulking rock. Arriving here much later than July 4 was not cause for celebration because it increased the risk of winter snows in the mountains at the end of the trail.

Many of the names carved or painted on the rock are still visible. Most names, however, have been destroyed by time and vandals. Nine bronze tablets have preserved some names, including missionaries Narcissa Prentiss Whitman and Eliza Hart Spalding. Another plaque memorializes Dr. Grace Raymond Hebard (1861-1936), a University of

Wyoming educator and administrator who was instrumental in preserving Wyoming landmarks and history, including the stories of Sacajawea and Esther Morris.

This roadside rest area has an excellent display with interpretive boards, photographs and trails, plus sheltered picnic tables. (307) 777-7695.

(11) DEVIL'S GATE (seven miles southwest of Independence Rock off State 220)

Emigrants passed below this pleasant viewing site, managed by the Bureau of Land Management. The menacing rock formations here mirrored the trail's danger. The emigrants often buried their dead up on this bluff, which was also an ancient Arapaho burial ground.

Two miles northwest of here is the infamous Martin's Cove, where nearly 150 members of a Mormon handcart company starved or froze to death in a November storm— four months later than was thought prudent. A rescuer described an agonizing scene:

> **There were old men pulling and tugging their carts, sometimes loaded with a sick wife or children, women pulling along sick husbands, little children six to eight years old struggling through the mud and snow.**

Many of these handcart pioneers were emigrants from the British Isles and Scandinavia, and many were very young or very old, and some quite sickly to begin with. They believed their faith would carry them through.

Unlike these unfortunate people, most handcart companies started their trek early enough in the year to make it through safely.

LANDER

(12) *Sacajawea grave and monument* (west of Fort Washakie on the Wind River Indian Reservation, 15 miles north of Lander on US 287. The pleasant town of Lander is a nine-mile detour from the turnoff from US 287 to Wyoming 28.)

Perhaps more monuments honor Sacajawea than any other American woman. Yet the teenager who aided the success of the 1804 Lewis and Clark expedition remains a mystery. Her true role in the trek that opened the west probably lies somewhere between that of legendary heroine and main expedition guide, and the young mother, cook and caretaker she was supposed to be.

Captured and gambled away as a slave to a rival Indian tribe, the young girl became the property of the old—and often drunk—French trapper Charbonneau. Carrying her infant son, Sacajawea opened communication with Indians along the way—including her long-lost brother, whom she encountered on the way in present-day Montana. She also rescued valuable equipment from a flooded canoe at one point, cared for the sick, and taught her fellow travelers uses of the wild plants and animals along the way.

Historians still don't agree where or when Sacajawea died. Some say she died within a few years of the Lewis and Clark expedition at Fort Manuel in South Dakota. Others claimed that she returned here to her adopted Shoshone people and died in 1884 when she was nearly 100 years old.

Inquire at tribal headquarters in Fort Washakie for directions and permission to visit the grave.

SOUTH PASS CITY

South Pass City Historic Site (about thirty-four miles south of Lander on Wyoming 28, then two miles southeast on a loop road)

South Pass City is by far the most interesting interpretive site between Lander and Farson, so be sure to take the loop road that leads to this evocative place.

Esther Morris cabin

(13) Esther Morris cabin (east side of town)

This restored village was a boisterous gold mining town when Esther Hobart Morris arrived here from Illinois with her sons and second husband in 1869. She was still smoldering from the indignity of being barred by law to inherit property from her first marriage. Nearly six feet tall and 180 pounds, this mighty woman, according to legend, held a tea party in her home, where she publicly extracted a promise from Wyoming Legislature candidate William Bright to support a woman suffrage bill. He was elected and kept his promise. The bill passed in 1869, making women in Wyoming territory the first in the nation officially allowed to vote and hold office.

Esther Morris became the first woman justice of the peace, a post she held until she slapped her husband with an assault charge and left town.

The reconstructed, furnished Esther Morris cabin pays tribute to the woman whose statue represents Wyoming, The Equality State, in the Capitol Rotunda in Washington, DC.

Visitors facilities are open daily 9-6 May 15-Oct 15. Free. (307) 332-3684.

SOUTH PASS SUMMIT

(14) South Pass Roadside Rest Area and (15) South Pass Overlook (Wyoming 28 about nine miles south of the South Pass turnoff)

These two sites are within a few miles of each other and straddle the South Pass summit. South Pass is one of the most poignant, important places on the Oregon Trail, but it takes imagination and patience to break through the lack of good roads and interpretive signs, and the confusion regarding the signs that are here.

Historians. credit Robert Stuart, an Astorian returning east in 1812, as the first white person to discover this important passage through the Rocky Mountains. Rather than the steep, craggy passage one would expect, it's a gentle saddle. The only way emigrants could tell they'd crossed the summit was that the water now ran west instead of east. They were now officially in what was Oregon Country.

The rest area (west side of highway) has a sign explaining the significance of South Pass for the Indians, trappers, emigrants, and miners. The overlook (east side of highway) gives a panoramic view of the pass with interpretive signs.

This is not where the emigrants crossed the summit. That's about an eight mile trip east of the highway on dirt roads. The turnoff is just south of the Sweetwater River near the summit. Purists who want to see the exact spot can follow Gregory Franzwa's excellent directions in *The Oregon Trail Revisited.* Here are two markers:

> **Oregon Trail marker. Ezra Meeker, an 1852 emigrant who returned as an old man to mark the trail, placed this stone marker here. It reads simply, "Old Oregon Trail 1843–57."**

> **Narcissa Whitman and Eliza Spalding marker (a few yards from Ezra Meeker's Oregon Trail marker). This two-foot-high slab marker honors the two intrepid missionary wives who crossed the continent in 1836. It reads "NARCISSA PRENTISS WHITMAN. ELIZA HART SPALDING. FIRST WHITE WOMEN TO CROSS THIS PASS JULY 4, 1836."**

(16) Parting of the Ways (a few miles south of the South Pass
Overlook, west side of the highway)

From the time they left their homes, parting became a
way of life for travelers on the Oregon Trail. They parted
with friends and family when they left home. They left
family and friends on the trail if they fell behind. They
parted with loved ones who died on the plains. From South
Pass on, wagon trains divided as cutoffs opened up. The
travelers would head for separate destinations—Oregon or
Salt Lake, or California.

So the fuss about which is the "true" Parting of the Ways
misses the point, because there was no true Parting of the
Ways. A lovely stone Parting of the Ways Monument marks
what is now known as the "False Parting of the Ways." It
tells of a fork in the trail—"right to Oregon, left to Utah
and California"—and lists among the travelers here
missionaries M. Whitman and H.H. Spalding. The monument mentions Narcissa Whitman and Eliza Spalding
merely as "and wives."

Parting of the Ways Monument

The "true" Parting of the Ways, according to signs, is about ten miles southwest of here. It's hard to find, and marked with a hand-painted stone. One can catch the mood of the various Partings of the Ways simply by gazing into the endless sagebrush prairie and imagining the sorrow of the partings, wherever and however they surely happened on the long westward journey.

FORT BRIDGER

(17) Fort Bridger State Historic Site and Museum (Business Loop 80)

Particularly in early years, most emigrants made a straight shot southwest from South Pass to Fort Bridger to replenish supplies, mail letters, and taste some semblance of "civilization" before hurrying on ever westward. Fort Bridger was a major Parting of the Ways, for after 1847, this was where Mormons and some California-bound travelers continued southwest on the Mormon Trail. Oregon-bound and other California travelers turned northwest toward Soda Springs and Fort Hall.

Mountain man Jim Bridger established Fort Bridger as a trading post in 1842. The Mormons ran it for a couple of years, then the army, and finally local settlers. The fort also served miners, lumbermen, ranchers, survey parties, the Overland Stage, the Pony Express, and the Union Pacific Railroad.

Judge William A. Carter built a commercial empire beginning with a trading post at the fort. Judge Carter's wife, Mary, carried on her husband's empire after his death. Sign boards near the Post Trader's Store mention Mary Carter's role in carrying on the business.

It was at Fort Bridger that the Donner party made the fateful decision to take the new Hastings cutoff to California in 1846. George Donner's wife, Tamsen opposed the new route, but, being a woman, such a decision was not hers to make.

On the advice of none other than Jim Bridger, the party turned southwest and took the cutoff. Half the Donner party died in Sierra winter storms before they were rescued eight months after leaving Fort Bridger. Among the living was little Patty Reed, who still had with her a lock of hair belonging to her grandmother, Sarah Keyes, who had died at Alcove Spring at the journey's beginning. (See Alcove Spring, Kansas.)

At Fort Bridger, there's an annual Labor Day Mountain Man Rendezvous—a bash reminiscent of the times mountain men and Indians would get together to trade goods and raise hell. Rendezvous are becoming popular entertainment not only throughout this country, but in parts of Europe.

The restored Fort Bridger is open daily 9-5 May 15-Oct, and weekends only the rest of the year. Small admission. (307) 782-3842.

BORDER

(18) Indian Grave (four miles west of Border)

There was humanity on the trail, sometimes between emigrant and Indian. The wife of an Indian chief was killed here in a fall from a horse in 1849. Aubrey Haines, in *Historic Sites Along the Oregon Trail*, recorded two emigrant men's reactions.

One watched her burial:

> **She was buried according to their custome.**
> **She was put into the ground & all her things**
> **were put with her, and an equal share of all**
> **their provisions. They then shot the horse and**
> **put him into the grave for the woman to ride.**
> **They then fired a few guns into the grave & put**
> **up a most piteous howling, weeping, and**
> **waleing—and in that state of agony departed**
> **from the place.**

Another emigrant wrote that her grave was marked with "a rude wooden cross, on which was pencilled:—'An Indian Squaw . . . , Kill'd by a fall from a horse, near this place: Calm be her sleep, and sweet her rest. Be kind to the Indian.'"

IDAHO

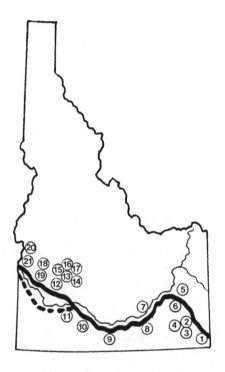

When Idaho became a state in 1890, artist and teacher Emma Edwards Green became the only woman to design a state seal. Her $100 prize design gave woman and man equal attention, reflecting the growing woman suffrage campaign, which would be won six years later. Mining, timber, wheat, the Snake River, and mountain grandeur illustrate the state's scenic and natural resources.

Voicing many early Idaho women's commitment to equality, Irene Welch Grissom, Idaho poet laureate from 1923 to 1948, wrote:

> **Go tell the world that the women give**
> **In an equal share with man!**

Idaho's name is attributed to a woman, according to Betty Penson-Ward, author of the delightful book *Women in Idaho History.* Luzena Brazelton Wallace, wife of the Idaho governor at statehood, is said to have named Idaho after her baby niece, Idaho Jackson.

There's a saying, Penson-Ward wrote, that of the thousands who crossed Idaho from 1843 to 1863, the only ones who stayed were those in graves. Gold discovery in 1862 brought fortune seekers back from Oregon and California, and Idaho became the first state to be settled from the west.

Idaho does a fine job celebrating its Oregon Trail history with reenactments, interpretive history, living history and Oregon Trail guides, including *Oregon Trail in Idaho* (map and brochure) and *Undisturbed in Idaho* (booklet). For information and brochures, contact Idaho Travel Council, 700 W. State St., Boise, ID 83720. 1-800-VISIT-ID.

The emigrants, after weeks of sage and dust, must have welcomed the sight of the wooded, grassy lands of what is now eastern Idaho. It was tough going, with the notorious Big Hill to cross. (Ruts can still be seen from Highway 30 east of Montpelier.) The road continued to be littered with abandoned wagons, dead oxen, graves, and dreams gone awry.

MONTPELIER
(1) Smith's Trading Post (five miles south of Montpelier)

A highway sign identifies the site of Peg Leg Smith's trading post near here. Stories abound about this character who traded in "cattle, whiskey, &c" at his store in 1849 and '50. Legend has it that he amputated his own leg after a bullet shattered it. Peg Leg, a sometime horse thief and trader, made good money, thanks largely to the unpaid work of his numerous Indian wives.

SODA SPRINGS
Soda Springs cemetery
(2) Wagonbox Grave

Danger from Indian attack rose in the mid-'50s and into the '60s, when Indians lost their lands to the whites. An ornate gravestone in the Soda Springs cemetery memorializes a family killed by Indians near here in 1861. Trappers and emigrants buried the father, mother and five children in their own wagon box.

(3) *Mary Christoffersen and Niels Anderson gravestone*

The large, stately gravestone in the serene parklike cemetery says simply "Anderson" on one side. The other side, in raised engraved letters, tells Mary and Niels' long, sad, and angry story of their involvement in what became known as the 1862 Morrisite Massacre in Utah. In the three-day confrontation between Morrisites and Mormon leadership, a cannonball shot off fourteen-year-old Mary's chin and killed two women, according to the gravestone.

Mary and Niels were among those who left Utah and settled near Soda Springs, where they married. Niels became known as the father of the anti-Mormon party in Idaho. The couple's eight children's names appear at the bottom of the gravestone tome, concluding with the words, "To father and mother, and historic to man, we dedicate this memorial."

(4) Soda Springs (just west of the town of Soda Springs)

Signs mark the area where emigrants marveled at the sight of the springs and geysers. Abigail Scott Duniway wrote of the Soda Springs:

> **They are a great curiosity: The first view we had was . . . two mounds of lime-stone rock. . . . The water boils up about one foot from the top of the wall; it is quite cool and when . . . sweetened, with the addition of a little vinegar, makes a drink equal to any prepared soda in the States.**

Most of the springs are now under water.

POCATELLO
(5) Old Fort Hall replica (Ross Park, 2900 block, South 4th Avenue)

Old Fort Hall replica

Nathaniel Wyeth built the original stockaded Fort Hall in 1834 for his fur trade. The Hudson's Bay Company put him out of business when it built Fort Boise farther to the west in the same year. Wyeth sold out to the HBC, which then encased the wood fort with adobe. Under the HBC, Fort Hall became a resting and wagon repair stop for Oregon Trail emigrants, who were by now two-thirds through their journey. The US took over the fort in 1855 mainly for protection of the emigrants.

The site of the original fort is fifteen miles northwest of here on the Shoshone-Bannock Indian Reservation. Dr. Minnie Howard of Pocatello led efforts to find the original site, and then to build a replica of Fort Hall. This remarkable woman was a teacher, a medical doctor, historian, founder of the local library, and mother of four sons.

Today, thanks to Dr. Minnie Howard, the replica of Fort Hall stands in Pocatello's Ross Park, a beautiful place for today's travelers to rest. Inside the fort, operated by the City of Pocatello, are restored shops, a restaurant and saloon. Local people demonstrate living history crafts in summer.

The replica is closed winter months. Hours vary. Admission charged. (208) 234-6233.

The Bannock County Historical Museum is across the road from the Fort Hall replica. Here, the visitor can learn about the Bannock-Shoshone Indians, who wintered in the meadows known as "The Bottoms" a few miles northwest of here, where the real Fort Hall once stood. Closed Dec 16-Jan 15. Hours vary. Admission charged. (208) 233-0434.

FORT HALL
(6) Fort Hall Indian Reservation

Sacajawea, the Shoshoni woman who traveled with Lewis and Clark, was from the Lemhi band of Shoshoni, which eventually settled here. The Shoshone and Bannock tribes were moved to the reservation with the 1868 Fort Bridger Treaty. At tribal headquarters, visitors can arrange to tour the reservation and see the site of old Fort Hall and other Oregon Trail sites, a large buffalo herd and the tribal museum. There's a tour charge, and reservations one day in advance are appreciated. (208) 238-3700.

AMERICAN FALLS
(7) Massacre Rocks State Park (10 miles southwest of Idaho Falls on I-86, westbound)

After the mid-1850s, in this menacing place they called "Gate of Death" and "Devil's Gate," the emigrants feared Indian attack more here than anywhere else. By then, emigrant traffic had ruined Indian trails and hunting grounds, and brought sickness and death. Small trains were especially vulnerable to Indian revenge.

Elizabeth Goltra wrote in 1853:

> **[W]e are now among the most hostile tribe of**
> **Indians on the route, many emigrants have**
> **been killed here, there should not be less than**
> **15 or 16 wagons together, we camped alone last**
> **night, but we kept a constant guard, we have**
> **not been troubled as yet, we will join some**
> **train the first one we come up with that suits.**

Interstate 86 parallels the stretch of trail where in 1862, Indians attacked several small wagon trains, killing ten people. Today, Massacre Rocks State Park features a nice visitor center, picnic area, campground, recreation facilities, trail walks, summer evening campfire programs and a stretch of wagon ruts. Camping and entrance fees. (208) 548-2672.

(8) Register Rock (2 miles south of Massacre Rocks State Park, most easily reached both directions from exit 28)

This half-buried boulder was another Kilroy-was-here spot, where emigrants carved or painted their names. A place of rest for the emigrants, it's a lovely rest and picnic stop for today's travelers as well.

MURTAUGH

(9) Cauldron Linn (about 2 miles east of Murtaugh off US 30)

Only a sign tells the traveler of a terrible stretch of the Snake where the 1811 Wilson Price Hunt party of Astorians capsized several canoes. No road leads to it now. Robert Stuart of the Hunt party wrote of the churning waters: "Hecate's Caldron was never half so agitated when vomiting even the most diabolical spells, as is this Linn . . ."

Linn is an old Scottish word meaning waterfall, hence, Cauldron Linn.

Stuart's reference to Hecate conjured up the most horrible image he could think of—that of an evil witch cackling over her diabolic brew. The meaning of Hecate and cauldron has changed since ancient times. Author Barbara Walker wrote that in ancient times, Hecate was revered as the wise woman Heqit, the Egyptian goddess of midwives. During the Middle Ages, religious authorities diabolized Hecate as the Queen of Witches when they deemed midwives dangerous and persecuted them as evil witches. In ancient times, the cauldron, rather than evil witches' brew, symbolized cyclical time or the cosmos.

HAGERMAN

(10) Thousand Springs (6 miles south of Hagerman off US 30)

Emigrants marveled at the sight of what looked like thousands of waterfalls cascading down the cliffs of the Snake River Canyon. The waters came partly from the Lost River, which disappeared into the ground more than 100 miles northeast of here. Here, Indians caught salmon and traded them with the emigrants.

Today, most of the twenty-five springs have been harnessed for hydro power and fisheries, but the remaining ones are still beautiful. The most spectacular of the falls is from Minnie Miller Spring, named for the pioneer dairy-woman who owned the Thousand Springs Farm.

Private recreation facilities flourish in this area, with few public facilities. The Idaho Nature Conservancy has preserved the 425-acre Thousand Springs Farm, which

Thousand Springs

provides sanctuary for waterfowl, eagles, owls, herons, and fish. Right here amidst the lush trees and grass and water is the grave marker of Idalia Edgemoor, Minnie Miller's favorite cow.

GLENNS FERRY

(11) Three Island Crossing State Park (I-84, exit 120, follow signs to park)

After crossing the Snake River numerous times, the emigrants had to decide whether to remain on the dry, rocky south bank of the Snake, or risk the dangerous crossing here at Three Island Ford. About half chose the crossing, using two of the three islands.

Elizabeth Wood wrote of the crossing in 1851:

> **We forded the Snake River, which runs so swift that the drivers (four to a team) had to hold on to the ox yokes to keep from being swept down by the current. The water came into the wagon boxes, and after making the island we raised the boxes on blocks, engaged an Indian pilot, doubled teams, and reached the opposite bank in safety. It is best in fording this river to engage a pilot.**

Fording was the only way to cross here until 1869, when Gus Glenn made the crossing easier—and more expensive—with his ferry.

Today, Three Island State Park is one of the most pleasant stops along the Oregon Trail, with a visitor center, campground, hiking, swimming and fishing, and an annual Crossing Reenactment in August. Open year-round. Camping and entrance fees. (208) 366-2394.

BOISE

Flood waters in the late nineteenth century wiped out traces of the Oregon Trail through Boise. It paralleled the Boise River on the south side, through what is now the Boise State University campus.

Military Reserve Park (Fort and Reserve streets)

(12) Fort Boise (not to be confused with the Hudson Bay Company's Fort Boise near Parma)

The army built Fort Boise in 1863 to protect emigrants and gold miners, and the city of Boise grew up around it. Two of the fort's buildings still stand and are part of the VA medical center in Military Reserve Park.

(13) O'Farrell Cabin

Irish immigrant Mary Ann Chapman O'Farrell lived here with her miner husband in Boise's first log cabin, built in 1863. Not only did she have seven children of her own, she also cared for seven orphan children—heroic deeds themselves. After she invited two Catholic priests on horseback to celebrate Mass, her cabin became a chapel as well.

O'Farrell Cabin

(14) Julia Davis, Ann Morrison, and Kathryn Albertson parks
(downtown Boise)

These parks are named for three benefactors of the Boise community. In the early 1900s, Canadian-born pioneer Julia McCrum Davis's family donated in her memory land along the riverside where the Oregon Trail went through the area. Women friends of Anna Daly Morrison donated trees for the park dedicated in her memory in the 1950s. Ann Morrison's world travels promoted world harmony as well as her husband's construction business (Morrison-Knudsen). Kathryn McCurry Albertson, of the Albertson supermarket family, is a contemporary community builder.

(15) Idaho Historical Society (610 Julia Davis Drive)

Gertrude McDevitt, director of the Historical Society in the 1940s and '50s, was instrumental in getting the museum in its present Julia Davis Park location. According to author Betty Penson-Ward, Gertrude McDevitt worried about the presence of a skeleton of an Indian woman in a glass case in the museum. McDevitt insisted that the skeleton be returned to her people. "But, you know," she told Penson-Ward, "for a long time I truly missed her."

Today, the Idaho State Historical museum has a fine collection of pioneer and Indian history, including such items as a gourd with a corncob stopper used to carry flax seed across the plains from Indiana about 1850. Open year-round. Free. (208) 334-2120.

(16) Mary Tolles memorial drinking fountain (City Hall)

Noticing that Boise had no place for people to get a drink of water except in a bar, prohibitionist Mary Tolles arranged for strategic placement of barrels of water downtown. The local WCTU dedicated a drinking fountain in her memory in 1910. The National Organization for Women restored the fountain in 1979, according to Betty Penson Ward.

(17) Clara Campbell Memorial Tree (Statehouse lawn, 8th and Jefferson)

Yes, there is a tree with a plaque on it dedicated to Clara Campbell, one of three women elected to the Idaho House in 1898, two years after Idaho women won the vote. Campbell, who sponsored legislation establishing the University of Idaho, promoted both woman suffrage and temperance as a pioneer legislator.

CALDWELL

(18) Ward Massacre Site (Lincoln Road, two miles south of Middleton off US 20)

A commemorative sign and state park picnic area now occupy the place of horror where Indians attacked and killed eighteen members of a small wagon train in 1854, leaving two survivors, both young boys. The killings fueled Indian-white fighting and forced the closure of Old Fort Boise that same year. Oregon Trail travel became even more dangerous in small groups and without military escort.

(19) Strahorn Library (Albertson College campus)

Carrie Adele Strahorn and her husband helped establish Caldwell in 1882 and worked to attract the railroad and settlers here. Carrie Strahorn was a founder of the town's Presbyterian Church, which was instrumental in founding the College of Idaho, now Albertson College. From her travels with her husband, Strahorn wrote the book *Fifteen Thousand Miles by Stage*, illustrated by the famous cowboy artist Charles Russell and published in 1911.

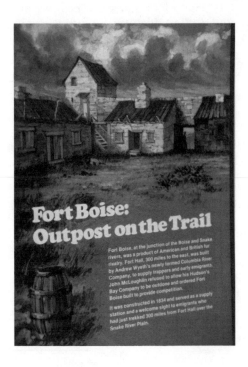

Fort Boise: Outpost on the Trail

Fort Boise, at the junction of the Boise and Snake rivers, was a product of American and British fur rivalry. Fort Hall, 300 miles to the east, was built by Andrew Wyeth's newly formed Columbia River Company, to supply trappers and early emigrants. John McLoughlin refused to allow his Hudson's Bay Company to be outdone and ordered Fort Boise built to provide competition.

It was constructed in 1834 and served as a supply station and a welcome sight to emigrants who had just trekked 300 miles from Fort Hall over the Snake River Plain.

PARMA

(20) Old Fort Boise (park east side of town)

This is a replica of the old trading post established in 1834 by the Hudson Bay Company to run Nathaniel Wyeth's Fort Hall out of business. Like Fort Hall, Old Fort Boise's original logs were covered with adobe. High water and Indian trouble forced the trading post to close in 1854. The original site is four miles northwest of Parma on the old Fort Boise Game Reserve.

Here is where westward-bound missionaries Marcus and Narcissa Whitman, and Henry and Eliza Spalding conducted Idaho's first church services when they passed through in 1836.

Campground, trailer facilities, showers are available. Hours vary. (208) 722-5573 or 5138.

Marie Dorion statue

(21) Marie Dorion statue

On the grounds of the Old Fort Boise replica stands a unique and charming statue of perhaps the bravest heroine in western history, the Iowa Indian Marie Dorion. The only woman member of the 1811 Wilson Price Hunt expedition to Astoria, she wintered with the trappers in a cabin near Parma during an 1813-1814 trapping expedition.

Bannock Indians killed the men, but the young mother escaped with her two young sons and a horse (some accounts say two horses). She set out for the Columbia River in the dead of winter. She crossed the Snake River, which she likely swam, probably somewhere near Farewell Bend. Marie Dorion with her children pressed on for nine days until a snow storm trapped the trio near the Blue Mountains. She built a hut of branches and snow and survived for nearly three months on berries, twigs, and, finally, her horse.

She crossed the Blue Mountains and reached a village of Walla Walla Indians near Meacham Creek, a Columbia tributary. Marie Dorion eventually remarried and settled in Oregon's Willamette Valley, where a small plaque marks the grave of this amazing woman. Her skills enabled her to survive hardships most emigrants could not.

WASHINGTON

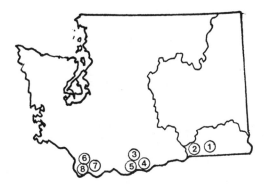

What is now Washington was part of the original Oregon Country, and emigrants began settling here as early as 1845. Although Washington is not part of the official Oregon Trail, the Whitman Mission, Fort Vancouver, and other Washington places played important roles in Oregon Trail history.

WALLA WALLA

(1) Whitman Mission National Historic Site (a few miles west of Walla Walla off US 12)

Here at Waiilatpu, the place of the people of the tall grass, Marcus and Narcissa Prentiss Whitman built their mission to the Cayuse Indians in 1836 after their amazing trek across the country, starting in New York. Narcissa and Marcus were determined to bring civilization to the "heathen" Indians. Narcissa supervised the school, instructed the girls in homemaking skills and taught hymns, while Marcus, a doctor, ministered to the Cayuse and tried to turn the nomadic people into farmers.

197

Marcus's trek to the East Coast to save the mission in 1842 and the Great Migration of 1843, which he led on his return, greatly increased the numbers of emigrants coming westward.

Narcissa didn't belong in this isolated place, where she lost her small child, her vision, her health, and ultimately her life. The Whitman Mission became a way-station for Oregon Trail emigrants, especially the sick and destitute. They brought measles and other diseases that white people could withstand but Indians could not.

The deaths of Indian children, but not white children, aroused Indian suspicions of a plot to wipe them out, igniting an attack on the mission in 1847. The Whitmans were among the victims. Shock waves from the massacre spread throughout Oregon Country, reduced the migration for a time, triggered a war between the settlers and the Indians, and led to creation of the Oregon Territory in 1848.

Today, the Whitman Mission is a lovely, peaceful place. Administered by the National Park Service, the grounds have a visitor center and an extensive trail system that leads to building sites, the great grave containing the remains of Narcissa and Marcus Whitman, and the Whitman Memorial at the top of the hill Narcissa used to climb to meditate. There's a picnic area, but no camping. Open daily. Contact: Superintendent, Rt. 2, Box 247, Walla Walla, WA 99362. (509) 529-2761. Admission charged.

Whitman Mission,
common grave

Two Sisters

WALLULA

(2) Two Sisters (a few miles south of Wallula on US 395/730)

An Indian legend grew around the two huge basalt pillars here. Coyote, the story goes, fell in love with three sisters who were building a trap in the river to catch salmon. Coyote watched them and each night, he would destroy their trap. Each day, the sisters would rebuild it. In a blatant case of sexual harassment, Coyote promised that if they would marry him, he would rebuild the trap and leave it alone. So they did and he did. They all lived happily until Coyote became jealous of his wives and turned two of them into these pillars and the other into a cave downstream. He then turned himself into a rock so he could keep an eye on his wives forever.

GOLDENDALE

(3) Maryhill Museum (about 12 miles south of Goldendale off Washington 14)

At this point, most of the emigrants were on the other side of the Columbia River making their way across the Columbia Plateau above the river.

Maryhill Museum has no Oregon Trail history, but it has American Indian history. The lives and passions of several women came together here, resulting in one of the most eclectic and fascinating museums anywhere. A queen's throne and ancient Indian stone carvings? You'll see them right here, 100 miles from a population center in what has been called "Castle Nowhere," the "loneliest museum in the world."

Roadbuilder Sam Hill built this massive structure as a "ranch house," with hopes of building a Quaker farming colony here. He named it Maryhill in honor of his wife and daughter, both named Mary, but the Quakers never came and the older Mary never liked the place. Through a web of friendships and associations too complicated to explain here, Maryhill now houses works of the French sculptor Auguste Rodin, including one of his lover, sculptor Claudine Claudel; a throne and personal effects of Queen Marie of Romania; art of dancer Loie Fuller; Russian icons; French glass; American Indian baskets; antique chess sets and French fashion mannequins.

Queen Marie dedicated the unfinished museum in 1926, largely out of gratitude for Hill's aid to Romania during World War I. Another friend, art collector Alma Spreckels, oversaw completion of the museum after Hill's death in 1931 and became the museum's principal benefactor.

Maryhill Museum has a little cafe with catering services, a museum store, and offers educational programs and rotating exhibitions. Admission is charged. Open daily 9-5 March 15-Nov 15. 35 Maryhill Museum Drive, Goldendale, WA 98620.

(4) Stonehenge (just east of State 14 and US 87 junction, east of Maryhill Museum)

So what the Sam Hill is a replica of Stonehenge doing in the Columbia Gorge? Sam Hill, builder of Maryhill and visionary with a Quaker background, built the replica in the mistaken belief that the original Stonehenge in England had been used for human sacrifice to pagan gods. He constructed the replica as a reminder that "humanity is still being sacrificed to the god of war."

According to recent scholarship, "pagan gods" referred to pre-Christian woman-centered religion, the same paganism that God and the prophets crusaded against in the Old Testament. Scholars believe that the original Stonehenge was built in stages, from about 2800 BC until after 1100

BC—more than seventeen centuries. Similar structures grew all over the British Isles and the Continent, used for village celebrations and rituals. You could say that they were the earliest cathedrals and observatories.

The early Stonehenge likely was associated with rituals of birth and death when people regarded the energy of the universe as female. Cycles of sun and moon were central to the belief system, so astronomy, spirituality and ritual intertwined.

She Who Watches

(5) *She Who Watches* (Tsagaglalal)

A widely-told legend tells of Coyote's journey up the river to the village, where he asks how the people are treated. Their chief, Tsagaglalal, who sits up on the rocks above the village, tells him that her people live well, eat well and live in strong houses. Coyote tells her that soon the world will change, and women will no longer be chiefs. He uses his magic and changes Tsagaglalal to stone. "You will stay there forever," he tells her, "and you will watch over your people."

She Who Watches is still there. The petroglyph (carving on rock) is one of a group believed to be more than 1500 years old. From her place somewhere on the rocks over the Columbia Gorge, she watches.

VANCOUVER

(6) Fort Vancouver (east off I-5 at Mill Plain exit, follow the signs to the visitor center)

The Hudson's Bay Company built Fort Vancouver in 1825 to establish British presence in the region, putting the imposing, white-haired Dr. John McLoughlin in charge as chief factor. The fort became the fur trade capital of the Pacific coast, an agricultural center, and a stopping place for weary and destitute Oregon Trail emigrants. Dr. McLoughlin was too kind to them for his own good, loaning them supplies and money, most never repaid.

Narcissa and Marcus Whitman and Eliza and Henry Spalding spent time here in glorious relief from their 1836 trek across the country to build missions to the Indians.

Fort Vancouver is now a National Historic Site administered by the National Park Service. The restored structures and visitor center are impressive, with living history interpretation on the 300-acre site. There's little evidence of the presence of women at Fort Vancouver, even though many of the fort's personnel had Indian wives, including Dr. John McLoughlin.

There's some mention of "servants," who were mostly Indian women. They served the men in the main dining room, then ate in the separate eating area designated for women.

The women were essential for the fur trade. They knew how to skin game and cure the skins and often accompanied the men on trapping brigades that could take up to a year.

According to a legend recorded in Bill Gulick's *Roadside History of Oregon*, it was the Indian women who planted the apple orchards in the area from seeds left on the dinner plates of Dr. McLoughlin's gentlemen guests.

Facilities include a visitor center, gift shop and site reconstructions. No picnic or camping facilities. Open daily 9-4, summer 9-5. Small admission. 612 East Reserve St., Vancouver, WA 98661. (206) 696-7655.

(7) The Academy (400 E. Evergreen)

Esther Pariseau grew up in Montreal and learned to build things from her father, Joseph. As Sister Joseph of the Sisters of Providence, she came west in 1856 and became the Mother Superior of her order. By 1858 Mother Joseph and the sisters had established—and helped build—Providence Academy to house a boarding school, hospital, asylum, home for the aged, orphanage and chapel.

Completed in 1874, Providence Academy was at the time the largest structure north of San Francisco.

Today, The Academy is mainly an office building. The magnificent Gothic-style chapel has been preserved and provides the setting for weddings. Mother Joseph herself carved parts of the chapel's altar and railing.

Under Mother Joseph's direction, the Sisters of Providence established eleven hospitals, seven academies, five Indian schools, and two orphanages throughout the Northwest. The American Institute of Architects named Mother Joseph the Pacific Northwest's first architect, and a statue of Mother Joseph now represents the state of Washington in Statuary Hall in Washington, DC.

(8) *Esther Short Park* (Colonial and Eighth Streets)

When a Hudson Bay authority confronted American settler Esther Short over her family's right to settle here in 1845, Esther strode up to the group's leader and slapped him in the face. The British never bothered her again.

In the park named after her stands a bronze statue of a mother guarding the three children clutching her skirts.

Pioneer Mother
Esther Short Park

OREGON

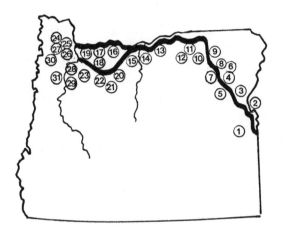

Oh Beulah Land, sweet Beulah Land
As on thy highest mount I stand:
I look away across the sea
Where mansions are prepared for me,
And view the shining glory shore—
My heaven, my home, forevermore.[1]
                —from "Beulah Land"

Some of the emigrants sang this hymn that envisions heaven, keeping before them the promise of Oregon. It hadn't been heaven up to now, and they still had a lot of hell to go through before they reached the Promised Land. After leaving the Snake River for several days the land was dry and threatening, with little fuel and water.

Watch for cedar kiosks that interpret state history at Oregon parks and highway rest areas. Local, state, and federal agencies and private companies tell the Oregon Trail story with exquisite illustrations and fine narrative. More interpretive sites are going up all the time.

State parks along the Oregon Trail don't take reservations and many fill up fairly early in the day during the summer. You can call ahead for information. Fees are charged for all state park camping sites and some day use areas. The Oregon State Park Campsite Information Center is at 1-800-452-5687 outside of Portland. In the Portland Metro area, call 238-7488. Many of the parks have their own phone numbers.

Excellent guides, including the *Oregon Trail Self Guided Tour Map* produced by the Oregon Trail Coordinating Council, are available through the Oregon Tourism Division. For publication and event information, contact the Oregon Tourism Division at 775 Summer St. NE, Salem, OR 97310. (800) 547-7842). Follow the map and the highway signs and have a fine time re-tracing the trail. Watch for Oregon Trail obelisks marking traces of the trail.

Like the other trail states, Oregon is whooping it up with Oregon Trail events. Spectacular interpretive centers blend with quiet, reflective places to contemplate the events of a century and a half ago. In that contemplation, we learn something of ourselves.

VALE
(1) Keeney Pass (southwest of Vale on Enterprise Avenue)
   Here you can see erosion-aided ruts sunk into the earth as the wagon trains narrowed their path to climb up this draw. Expect to see a new interpretive display with hiking trails at this Bureau of Land Management site.

HUNTINGTON

(2) Farewell Bend State Park (southeast of Huntington; 25 miles northwest of Ontario off I-84)

Here, emigrants said good-bye, not to other travelers, but to the Snake River, which had been their traveling companion off and on for hundreds of miles.

It's no wonder this was one of the most popular resting places along the Oregon Trail. It's lovely—one of my favorites too.

Both primitive and electrical camp sites, picnic, fishing, boating, swimming (chilly), showers, Oregon Trail exhibit. (503) 869-2365.

(3) Weatherby Rest Area (about 10 miles north of Huntington, I-84)

After the Burnt River Canyon, the emigrants faced a five- to six-day climb out of the canyon. The information panels here quote a journal entry by Wilson Price Hunt, leader of the 1811 party of Astorians. Hunt wrote about a woman who gave birth to a child after a harrowing trip over the mountains. She

> **. . . rode horseback with her newly born child in her arms. Another child, two years old and wrapped in a blanket, was fastened by her side. One would have thought, from her behavior, that nothing had happened to her.**

Although not named in the exhibit, the woman mentioned was the only woman on the Wilson Price Hunt expedition, the Iowa Indian Marie Dorion. The birth event took place east of North Powder.

BAKER CITY

(4) National Historic Oregon Trail Interpretive Center (Flagstaff Hill, five miles east of Baker City off Oregon 86)

At this point, the emigrants could see trees and green after seemingly endless dust and mud and sage. At the top of Flagstaff Hill, you can see this dramatic transition as you enter the National Historic Oregon Trail Interpretive Center.

If you don't make any other stop along the Oregon Trail, stop here. Opened with a grand celebration in May 1992, the 20,000-square-foot Interpretive Center has been attracting throngs of wide-eyed visitors ever since. The US

Bureau of Land Management operates the $10 million complex, a result of local, state and federal partnerships.

In astonishing detail, the Oregon Trail story unfolds in displays, videos, and re-creations of the Oregon Trail. Sounds and even smells accompany the trail and camp scenes. Interactive displays, living history, stage productions, outdoor programs, and walks along an extensive trail system take you on a journey that's as close as you can get to the real thing.

What makes it so authentic is the obvious presence of women and children with the men. Women were prominent in designing and interpreting this center, and it shows.

"It's an opportunity for people to understand that women were there," says BLM archeologist Mary Oman. "There's a sense of the human aspect—things that everyone can understand."

In addition to the Oregon Trail, other themes here are mining, explorers and fur traders, natural history, Native American history, and the general land office (forerunner of the Bureau of Land Management).

Gift shop. Open daily 9-4. Extended summer hours. Donations accepted. PO Box 987, Baker City, OR 97814, (503) 523-1843.

(5) *The Oregon Trail Regional Museum* (Campbell and Grove Streets)

Come see the three-ton Old Woman!

This Old Woman happens to be the second-largest meteorite ever found in the US, weighing in at more than 6,000 pounds—right here in eastern Oregon. The Old Woman Meteorite found its way from California to Oregon to join a magnificent collection of minerals and rocks, several collected and donated by women.

The world-class Cavin Collection of minerals, rocks and gems comes from sisters Elizabeth Cavin Warfel and Mamie Cavin, who found much of their collection in the Baker area. The sisters cut and polished many of their treasures themselves.

The Oregon Trail Regional Museum houses an extensive display of local and regional artifacts, including wagons, stage coaches, hand tools, and items from the local filming of the movie *Paint Your Wagon*.

Open April-November 9-4. Donations requested. (503) 523-9308.

NORTH POWDER
(6) Marie Dorion Marker (State 237 between North Powder and Union)

This marker notes that "in this vicinity a son was born to Madame Pierre Dorion 'the Madonna of the Old Oregon Trail'" although she traveled through here thirty years before the Oregon Trail's beginning. At this point in the 1811 Wilson Price Hunt Astoria expedition, the people were starving and had killed and eaten their horses except for the one Marie Dorion and her children rode.

After her baby was born, the Iowa Indian woman and her husband and children rested for a day. Within twenty-four hours after giving birth, Marie Dorion rode twenty miles on horseback and walked another twelve. The baby, born tiny and weak because of its mother's malnutrition, died eight days later.

LA GRANDE

Emigrants remarked on the spectacular beauty of this place in the middle of the Grande Ronde Valley. The Oregon Trail skirted the southwest edge of what is now La Grande.

(7) Hilgard Junction State Park (about eight miles north of La Grande off I-84)

Along the Oregon Trail, you'll frequently see information about the western explorer John C. Fremont, quoted here. His wife, Jessie, was probably one of the least-recognized influences on the westward movement. Jessie Fremont's father, Thomas Hart Benton, promoted migration to Oregon, and had an Oregon county named after him. Enthusiastic public response to John Fremont's published accounts of his 1842 and 1843 treks into Oregon Country helped fuel Oregon Fever, but the reports wouldn't have happened without Jessie Fremont, who is credited with turning her husband's rather dull narration into fascinating tales. To my knowledge, Jessie Fremont herself never set foot in Oregon Country.

Emigrants rested among the trees beside the Grande Ronde River at the site of this state park. Full hook-up plus tent sites, picnic, Oregon Trail exhibit, river rafting access.

Blue Mountain Crossing

MEACHAM
(8) Oregon Trail-Blue Mountain Crossing Interpretive Park
(Spring Creek Road exit south of Meacham. Three-mile access road.)

Here, emigrants neared the summit of the Blue Mountains—the most difficult crossing yet. "The hills here are all covered with fine timber," wrote Elizabeth Wood in 1851. "Some of them are awful steep, however."[2]

Stroll along a path beside 150-year-old wagon ruts at this interpretive park, planned for opening in summer 1993. In partnership with the Oregon Trail Coordinating Council and the National Guard, the US Forest Service recreates the trail's mood with gallery-quality paintings, thoughtful commentary and a radio broadcast soundtrack of a wagon train. Wheelchair-accessible trail, picnic area, shelter, restrooms.

(9) Squaw Creek Viewpoint (Mt. Emily Road exit)

Here's another of several Squaw Creeks and Squaw Mountains along the Oregon Trail, after the derogatory name the emigrants called American Indian women, not realizing that the ancient meaning of "squaw" was "queen" or "chief."

(10) Emigrant Springs State Park (north of Meacham, 26 miles southeast of Pendleton off I-84)

The Oregon Trail exhibit here is another elegant mix of evocative art and writing that capture the mood of the Oregon Trail: the weather extremes, exhaustion, death of animals and people. A beautiful painting shows a woman in a wagon led by an ox and a mule. By now it wasn't unusual to mix animals for wagon teams. The emigrants used whatever animals they had left.

Emigrant Springs State Park has facilities for full hook-ups and tents, group picnic shelter and meeting hall. (503) 983-2277.

PENDLETON

(11) Confederated Tribes Interpretive Institute (six miles east of Pendleton)

Many of the emigrants couldn't have made it that last stretch over the Cascades and down the Columbia River if it hadn't been for the help of the people already living here. The emigrants—however inadvertently—brought death and disease to many and destruction of the native people's way of life. Yet the people live and have much to teach.

The Confederated Tribes of Cayuse, Umatilla, and Walla Walla Indians plan to open the $12 million interpretive institute in 1995. It will examine the effects of the Oregon Trail migration on the tribes and the environment, as well as American Indian life before the migration and into the future. Two critical aspects of the interpretation are the changed environment of the area, and the impact of the European-introduced horse, which greatly affected the status of women.

"It will be a holistic interpretation," according to Jackie Cook, Institute Curator, focusing on "who we were, who we are, and who we will be."

For information, contact the Department of Community and Economic Development of the Umatilla Tribe. (503) 276-3873.

Rhoda and Ella Lazinko thrilled crowds
with their daring in relay races.
Courtesy of Pendleton Round-Up

(12) *Pendleton Round-Up Grounds and Pavilion* (1205 SW Court)

The famous Pendleton Round-Up takes place every September where the Oregon Trail passed through the area. The Pendleton community is paying increasing attention to its Oregon Trail heritage, with living history demonstrations and exhibits here at the Round-Up grounds. The Confederated Tribes of Cayuse, Umatilla, and Walla Walla Indians are prominent in the living history interpretations.

The Pendleton Round-Up Hall of Fame honors the cowboys, cowgirls, and community leaders who have contributed to the celebration since its beginning in 1910.

Women were active in the Round-Up from the beginning, in cowgirl parades, cowgirl bands, and especially in rodeo trick riding, relay racing, bronco riding, steer roping, and bulldogging. Women's rodeo participation waned following Bonnie McCarroll's death after a bucking horse threw her and fell on her in 1929. Because of McCarroll's death, the board of directors banned bucking events for women. But not for men.

Women still compete in rodeo relay and barrel racing. Pendleton Round-Up history photos reveal women's active rodeo participation fading after the 1920s, replaced by both Anglo and American Indian women's increasing visibility as queens and promoters.

For information on the Round-Up and Hall of Fame, contact the Round-Up Association, PO Box 609, Pendleton, OR 97801. (503) 276-2553. (800) 524-2984.

CELILO
(13) Celilo Park

Celilo Falls were the fishing grounds of Tsagalalal's people. Into the 1950s, the men would catch plentiful leaping salmon with dip nets from platforms built high over the raging waters of Celilo Falls. In a poignant passage in his novel *Winterkill*, Oregon author Craig Lesley described the flooding of the Celilo fishing grounds when the government built the Dalles Dam.

> **Then I heard a high wail. It was even louder than the roar of the falls. All the old Celilos had turned their backs to the rising water and were lined up facing the canyon wall. Their arms were crossed and they were chanting the falls' death chant.**
>
> **The lake rose against the falls. The water kept pouring over the falls, but the more it crashed into the lake, the higher the lake rose, choking it back. I closed my eyes, praying it would stop. . . .**
>
> **As the noise from the falls died, the wailing grew louder, like a shriek. One of the reservation chiefs . . . walked away . . . and joined the old men and women with their backs turned to the dark water. He was crying when he passed us, and he said, 'We sold our mother, and now they have drowned her.'[3]**

(14) Deschutes River Crossing, Deschutes River State Park (just east of Celilo on a side road off I-84)

The emigrants descended the slopes to the southeast and likely saw the Columbia River for the first time. They crossed the Deschutes River, floating what was left of the wagons, and swimming what were left of the livestock. Indians would ferry women and children across in canoes in exchange for brightly-colored shirts or anything else the emigrants might have left to trade.

> **. . . crossed falls or Shutes river it was high rapid and dangerous the water came clear to the top of the waggon beds me and my children with as many more women and children as could stow them selves in to a canoe was taken over by two indians which cost a good many shirts . . .**
>
> —Elizabeth Dixon Smith, 1847

The park has an extensive hiking and biking trail, fishing, primitive camp sites and Oregon Trail exhibit. (503) 739-2322.

Deschutes River Crossing

THE DALLES

Until 1845, when Sam Barlow forged a "road" around the south side of Mount Hood, The Dalles (French for narrow rapids) was the end of the land journey of the Oregon Trail. The emigrants had no choice but to take their chances on the raging Columbia on crude rafts or Indian canoes or bateaux (flat-bottomed boats). Many abandoned what was left of their wagons; others took the wheels off their wagons and put them on the rafts.

Pioneer Woman grave, near The Dalles

Nov 2 we took off our wagon wheels layed
them on the raft placed the wagon beds on
them and started . . . on 12 logs 18 inches
through and 40 ft long the water runs 3 inches
over our raft.
Nov 3 we are floating down the Columbia
cold and disagreeable weather.
                              —Elizabeth Dixon Smith, 1847

Methodist missionary Daniel Lee had started a mission here in 1838, without much success, but the settlement grew and became a life-saving stop for the emigrants. Fort Dalles, originally Camp Drum, protected emigrants and settlers and became a major supply station for the emigrants from 1850 through the 1860s.

The Dalles has preserved much of its history, which you can stroll through on a walking tour of this picturesque town.

The Dalles Convention and Visitor Bureau is at 901 East Second Street, The Dalles, OR 97058. (800) 255-3385 or (503) 296-6616.

(15) Gorge Discovery Center and Crates Point (just west of The Dalles on the Columbia River)

Edward and Sophia Crate arrived in The Dalles in 1849 and received the first wife-husband Donation Land Claim certificate in the area: 320 acres for her, 320 acres for him. They raised fourteen children and Edward ferried emigrants, soldiers, and supplies between The Dalles and Fort Vancouver.

Here, where the emigrants set off on their water journey down the Columbia, is where the Gorge Discovery Center is scheduled to open in 1996. A local-county-federal partnership, the center will interpret the environment and history of the area, including the Oregon Trail.

HOOD RIVER

Early settlers called this place "Dog River" after the meat they had to eat, but Mary Taylor White Coe changed the name to Hood River.

Pioneer Woman
Hood River County
Museum
Hood River, OR

(16) Hood River County Historical Museum (Port Marina Park)

This is a charming museum, with evocative displays of early Hood River Valley life and history. The reference center holds family histories of local pioneers.

The Pioneer Woman Sculpture

Amazingly, this sculpture, which looks like bronze, is paper mache. The sculptor, Aatto Annala, modeled it after his mother, Hilma Fredrieka Jampsa Annala, a native of Finland and pioneer in South and North Dakota in the 1890s. The flower she holds symbolizes the pioneer woman's awareness of and search for beauty amidst hardships.

Beadwork of Martha Alick

"Indian Martha" Alick was a healer and story teller whose stories of her people were recorded in the book *Legends of the Klickitats.*

Model of *The Mary*

Upstairs is a model of the steamboat *Mary*, built by Roger Attwell and named after his wife, Mary Hervy Williams Attwell, who crossed the plains in 1852. On her journey across the plains, Mary had lost her husband to cholera and two of her four-horse wagon team to Indians.

The *Mary* was part of the river transport system that grew along the Columbia beginning in the 1850s. The transportation web included sailboats, scows, barges and a wooden railroad for transporting supplies while passengers walked over the unnavigable part of the Columbia River at the Cascade rapids.

The *Mary* ran between the Dalles and the Cascades, and played a major role in evacuating pioneers to The Dalles in the 1856 Indian attack.

Engine Mary

The *Mary*'s steam engine is on display outside the museum.

The museum is open mid-April to end of October Wed-Sun 10-4. Donations welcome. (503) 386-6772.

CASCADE LOCKS

Some early emigrants lost their belongings, some their lives, trying to shoot the rapids here instead of portaging around the Columbia Cascades, where the "Great Shute" dropped twenty feet in 400 yards.

Columbia River Cascades

(17) *Bridge of the Gods*

According to an Indian legend, a natural land bridge once spanned the Columbia Gorge here, about where the steel truss bridge links Washington and Oregon today. Two gods, Pahto (Mt. Adams) and Wy'East (Mt. Hood), fought over the goddess (some versions say maiden) Mt. St. Helens. The two gods exploded, hurling fire and rocks over the land and water, collapsing the land bridge. Mt. St. Helens, the center of all this commotion, exploded centuries later in 1980.

(18) *Sternwheeler Columbia Gorge* (Cascade Locks Marine park)

Captain Minnie Hill's portrait joins those of early steamboat captains. Captain Hill learned how to navigate and handle a boat from her husband and, in 1886, became the first licensed woman steamboat captain west of the Mississippi.

The Sternwheeler offers day and evening excursions on the Columbia, June through early October from Cascade Locks, (503) 374-8427. Weekends October-May from Portland, (503) 223-3928.

(19) ***Crown Point State Park*** (about six miles west of Multnomah Falls on scenic byway)

Vista House, built in 1918 as a memorial to Oregon's pioneers, provides a spectacular view from high above the Columbia Gorge. Inside the National Historic Landmark building is a plaque commemorating the Iowa Indian heroine Marie Dorion. Gift shop, gallery and historical and environmental displays. Open daily May-Oct 15. (503) 695-2230.

BARLOW ROAD

In 1845 Sam Barlow and Joel Palmer just barely made it around the south side of Mount Hood to the Willamette Valley, opening an alternative route to floating the Columbia River. The next year, Barlow opened a toll "road," which proved just as hazardous as the river, with its steep grades and threatening snows.

The US Forest Service provides an excellent map, *The Barlow Road: Historic Oregon Trail*, with explanation and location of Barlow Road sites. US 26 parallels the Barlow Road in many places. Watch for signs showing ruts and swales.

GOVERNMENT CAMP

(20) Pioneer Woman's Grave (3/4 mile west of Barlow Pass Summit, off US 26)

A highway survey crew in 1924 discovered a rock cairn covering a wagon box coffin of an emigrant woman. Since then, people have added rocks to the grave site, honoring the memory of this unidentified woman resting in peace in a grove of trees. On the day I visited, someone had placed a flower on the grave.

Pioneer Woman's
grave

(21) Timberline Lodge (1 mile east of Government Camp, 7 miles off US 26)

Women played important roles in the design and making of the magnificent Timberline Lodge, built by the Works Progress Administration and the US Forest Service in 1936-37. Margery Hoffman Smith directed the interior design and Gladys Everett directed the WPA Women's and Professional Projects' weaving and sewing of the fabric decorating the inside. Rachel Griffin, charter member of Friends of Timberline, initiated the Exhibition Center, where a bust of her likeness can be seen in the Center in the lower lobby. Wood carvings in the main lobby honor pioneer and American Indian mothers.

A National Historic Landmark administered by the Forest Service, the lodge houses and elegantly feeds skiers and hikers year-round. (503) 231-7979.

(22) Laurel Hill (four miles west of Government Camp off US 26)

A sign off US 26 marks a short trail to the most prominent chute down Laurel Hill. The emigrants must have gotten dizzy just peering down this hill. They had to lower what was left of their wagons with ropes lashed around trees and pray the ropes didn't break. A new trail built by US Forest Service crews leads to the top of Laurel Hill.

RHODODENDRON

(23) Tollgate Campground (just east of Rhododendron)

A replica of the west tollgate stands serenely in this US Forest Service campground, where emigrants passed

West Tollgate replica
Barlow Road

through the fifth and final tollgate on the Barlow Road. Widows went through free, and men grumbled about paying yet another toll they couldn't afford for the "privilege" of using this treacherous path someone had the nerve to call a road. The road is prominent through the gate.

PORTLAND
(24) Oregon Historical Society (1230 SW Park Ave.)

Scenes depicted in two murals towering above the Oregon Historical Society's buildings in downtown Portland include Sacajawea with her infant child, and emigrants' wagons.

Inside are exhibits on Oregon history, including the Oregon Trail, American Indian culture, and Abigail Scott Duniway's relentless efforts for woman suffrage. The OHS library has a rich collection of manuscripts, journals and photographs from the Oregon Trail and settlement.

Gift shop and book store. Admission. Open Mon-Sat 10:00-4:45. (503) 222-1741.

(25) Abigail Scott Duniway Memorial (Johns Landing, 5331 SW Macadam Avenue)

It's a different kind of memorial, the likeness of Oregon suffragist Abigail Scott Duniway, at the top of the elevator tower at Johns Landing. The woman who lost her mother and young brother during the family's Oregon Trail passage in 1852 became the state's leading suffragist. She founded *The New Northwest*, a women's rights newspaper, and worked for forty-two years to win the right to vote for women in Oregon. Her most formidable opponent in the struggle was her own brother, Harvey W. Scott, powerful editor of *The Oregonian*. When she finally won, Abigail cast the first women's vote in Oregon. She was nearly eighty years old.

(26) Sacajawea statue (Washington Park, short distance from north entrance)

The lovely statue among the trees honors the Shoshone Indian woman who helped guide explorers Meriwether Lewis and William Clark to the Pacific in 1805. Some historians say Lewis—and especially Clark—saw the importance of having Sacajawea along and took her husband, the "lazy rascal" French Canadian trapper

Charbonneau, only because they had to. Yet Charbonneau was the one who got the money. With her infant son on her back, the teenaged Indian woman served as cook, nurse, hunter, peacemaker with Indians, and occasional guide.

Oregon historian Eva Emery Dye solicited money from women throughout the West for the Washington Park statue. During the 1905 Lewis and Clark Exposition, famous suffragists gathered to dedicate the statue, including Susan B. Anthony, Dr. Anna Howard Shaw, Carrie Chapman Catt, and Oregon's own Abigail Scott Duniway.

Dr. Shaw paid tribute to the young Shoshone woman:

> **Forerunner of civilization, great leader of men, patient and motherly woman, we bow our hearts to do you honor! . . . May we the daughters of an alien race . . . learn the lessons of calm endurance, of patient persistence and unfaltering courage exemplified in your life, in our efforts to lead men through the Pass of justice, which goes over the mountains of prejudice and conservatism to the broad land of the perfect freedom of a true republic; one in which men and women together shall in perfect equality solve the problems of a nation that knows no caste, no race, no sex in opportunity, in responsibility or in justice! May 'the eternal womanly' ever lead us on![4]**

(27) St. Vincent Hospital (9205 SW Barnes Road)

The contributions of Catholic nuns to the literal building of the Northwest have been given far too little attention, but St. Vincent Hospital helps to right the record. Inside the reception lounge is a portrait of Mother Emilie Gamelin, Canadian founder of the Sisters of Providence in 1847. A photo essay in an adjacent hall honors the Sisters of Providence who founded St. Vincent, including Mother Joseph, who designed the building and supervised its construction; Mother Mary Theresa, the hospital's first administrator; and Mother Gamelin.

On the second floor just outside the chapel is a replica of the statue of Mother Joseph, with her carpenter's tools, that represents the state of Washington in the Capitol rotunda in Washington, DC.

Mother Joseph
St. Vincent Hospital
Portland, OR

OREGON CITY
(28) End of the Oregon Trail Museum (5th and Washington)
and **End of the Oregon Trail Interpretive Center** (Abernethy
Green, corner of Abernethy and Washington)
   The delightful End of the Oregon Trail Museum is to
combine with the grand new End of the Oregon Trail
Interpretive Center, scheduled to open in 1995–1996.
Meanwhile, a Preview Center is to open in 1993. The
Preview Center, resembling gigantic covered wagons, will
contain an exhibit center, a high-tech movie theatre, and
an old-time mercantile store. Contact The Oregon Trail
Foundation, P.O. Box 511, Oregon City, OR 97045-0511.

(29) McLoughlin House National Historic Site (713 Center
Street, at the top of the street elevator)
   As Chief Factor of the Hudson Bay's Fort Vancouver,
John McLoughlin extended credit and supplies to the

incoming Americans. Largely due to his kindness, the Americans established a strong enough presence to extend US claim clear to the Canadian boundary. With that, McLoughlin was forced to retire his position; he renounced his British citizenship and became an American citizen. Many of the people he befriended did not return his kindness, but after his death the Oregon legislature properly named John McLoughlin "The Father of Oregon."

The elegant McLoughlin House contains personal effects of Dr. McLoughlin and his wife, Margaret Wadin McLoughlin, who was one-half Chippewa Indian.

Open Tues-Sat 10-4, Sun 1-4. Admission charged. (503) 656-2866.

FOREST GROVE
(30) Pacific University Museum (2043 College Way)

Tabitha Brown was sixty-six when she came on the Oregon Trail with members of her family, driving her own ox team. On the advice of a "rascally fellow," the party took the Applegate Cutoff through what is now northern California and southern Oregon. Lost and alone in the desert with her ill brother-in-law, the intrepid heroine nearly starved. She survived the ordeal and went on to start a glove-making business from a coin she found in her glove. With missionary Harvey Clark, the woman now known as "The Mother of Oregon" founded the Oregon Orphan Asylum, incorporated in 1849 into the new Tualatin Academy, which became what is now Pacific University.

Old College Hall, where Tabitha Brown once taught, is now a museum containing some of "Grandma Brown's" memorabilia and a portrait of her, painted by one of her descendants. This venerable museum also has displays and information on missionary and amateur botanist Mary Richardson Walker, whose photograph's dour expression reflects her hard life; Josephine Walker, Mary's daughter and pioneer missionary to China; and the Forest Grove Indian Training School, where Indian girls were taught Anglo ways of sewing, cooking, and doing laundry.

Also on campus are an arts building named after Tabitha Brown, a petrified tree stump marking the original location of Tualatin Academy, and a stone monument memorial to pioneer women.

Open Tues-Fri 1-4 Sept-May. Open by appointment in summer. (503) 357-6151, Ext. 2455

(31) CHAMPOEG (pronounced shamPOOee) **STATE PARK**
(between I-5 and OR 219 along the Willamette River)

This is where French-Canadian and American pioneer
men met to create Oregon's provisional government in
1844. The expansive state park, populated by resident
sheep, is a beautiful spot, with a campground, picnic sites,
ball fields and hiking and biking trails.

Admission charge to most facilities. (503) 678-1251.

Visitor Center: Interesting, but virtually no evidence of
women's presence.

Robert Newell House Museum (west of the park entrance)

Mountain man and early settler Robert Newell, with his
friend, Joe Meek, brought the first wagon into the
Willamette Valley in 1841. This house is a restoration of
the original, built in 1852, and contains pioneer and
American Indian artifacts, quilts and needlework. Its best-
known collection is the Oregon governors' wives' inaugura-
tion gowns. (It does not include the inaugural garb of
Senator Frank Roberts, Oregon's first husband of a
governor.) Also on the grounds are an old jail and a one-
room schoolhouse.

Kitty Newell grave

In a lovely area beside Champoeg Creek is the simple
gravestone of Kitty Newell, first wife of Robert Newell. The
daughter of a Nez Perce chief, Kitty Newell died in 1845.

DAR Cabin

This replica of a pioneer cabin replaced original homes
wiped away by floods in 1892. The charming house
contains many early pioneer artifacts and authentically-
furnished rooms.

ACKNOWLEDGMENTS

The following have provided valuable information and assistance:

The Academy, Vancouver, WA
Bear River State Information Center, Evanston, WY
The Central Exchange, Kansas City, MO
Children's Mercy Hospital, Kansas City, MO
David C. Duniway
End of the Trail Museum, Oregon City, OR
Historic Ward-Meade Park, Topeka, KS
Hood River County Museum, Hood River, OR
Idaho Division of Travel Promotion, Boise, ID
Idaho State Historical Museum and Kris Major, Boise, ID
Idaho State Historical Society, Boise, ID
Kansas Department of Commerce & Housing, Topeka, KS
Kansas State Historical Society
La Grande Ranger District, Wallowa-Whitman National Forest, La
    Grande, OR
Lane County Historical Society, Eugene, OR
Library of Congress Folk Life Center, Washington, DC
Maryhill Museum of Art, Goldendale, WA
Multnomah County Library, Portland, OR
National Frontier Trails Center, Independence, MO
National Historic Oregon Trail Interpretive Center, Baker City, OR
North Platte/Lincoln County Convention & Visitors Bureau, North
    Platte, NE
Oregon Historical Society, Portland, OR
Oregon Tourism Division
Oregon Trail Coordinating Council
Oregon Trail Foundation
Oregon Trail Regional Museum, Baker City, OR
Pacific University Museum, Forest Grove, OR
Pendleton Round-Up, Pendleton, OR
Soda Springs Public Library, Soda Springs, ID
St. Vincent Hospital, Portland, OR
Tigard Library, Tigard, OR
Jim Tompkins
The Wagner Perspective, Cheyenne, WY
Washington State University Library, Pullman, WA
Barbara Westmoreland

CREDITS

I wish to acknowledge a treasure of women's diaries, letters and reminiscences: *Covered Wagon Women*, a nine-volume series by Kenneth L. Holmes, published by the Arthur H. Clark Company.

I have drawn extensively from Dr. Holmes' transcription of the writing and reminiscences of Keturah Belknap, Amelia Stewart Knight, the Scott sisters and Elizabeth Dixon Smith (Geer), as well as others cited. For that privilege, I thank Dr. Holmes and Arthur H. Clark Company for their contribution and cooperation.

A note about Keturah Belknap, whose writing captivated me from the beginning. Material from her marriage through the end of her journey is from Washington State University, Pullman, Washington, as it appears in Holmes. Material from before her marriage is from Cathy Luchetti's *Women of the West* (Antelope Island Press, 1982). Material from after her settlement in Oregon is from "Ketturah Belknap's Chronicle of the Bellfountain Settlement," edited by Robert Moulton Gatke in the *Oregon Historical Quarterly* (September 1937).

Permission has been granted to quote material from the following diaries, journals, and reminiscences.

Belknap, Keturah. "Original Diary of Kitturah Penton (Mrs. George) Belknap [from Ohio to Fort Hall, Idaho, 1839 (sic)]" is in the Washington State University Libraries, Pullman, Washington.

Geer, Elizabeth Dixon Smith, Papers. Oregon Historical Society, Mss. 641.

Goltra, Elizabeth. "The Oregon Trail Diary of Elizabeth Goltra, 1853." Typed by Alice Pitney Norris. Oregon City, OR, 1988. "Journal of Travel Across the Plains, 1853." Lane County Historical Society, 1970.

Knight, Amelia Stewart. "Diary of an Oregon Pioneer of 1853." Transactions of The Oregon Pioneer Association, 1928, 38-56.

Maynard, Jane. Diary, 1867. MS 590, Katherine Tyler Hunt Collection, Idaho State Historical Society, Boise, ID.

Scott (Duniway), Abigail Jane, Catherine Scott (Coburn) and Mary Frances Scott (Cook), Scott family papers, David C. Duniway.

Stewart, Agnes. "The Diary of Agnes Stewart, 1853." From the Original Diary, Owned by Mr. Ivan Warner, Salem, OR. Courtesy of Eugene, OR: The Lane County Pioneer-Historical Society, 1959, 1966.

Stewart, Helen. "Diary of Helen Stewart, 1853." Courtesy of Eugene, OR: The Lane County Pioneer-Historical Society, 1961.

Warner, Elizabeth Stewart. Letter, 1856 or 1857, published with Diary, 1853, Agnes Stewart. Courtesy of Eugene, OR: Lane County Historical Society, 1959.

I gratefully acknowledge permission to reprint from the following:

"Overland 1852," a song by Linda Allen, ©1986. From the album *October Roses*, available from Rainbow Dancer Productions, PO Box 5881, Bellingham, WA 98227.

"What We Left Behind," a song from the musical play and recording *Voices from the Oregon Trail*, Copyright ©1991 by Marv Ross, Troutdog Music.

Pioneer Woman, a long poem by Pat McMartin Enders, Clackamas Press, 21730 SE Hiway 224, Clackamas, OR 97015.

Women's Diaries of the Westward Journey by Lillian Schlissel.

Winterkill by Craig Lesley.

Women and Men on the Overland Trail by John Mack Faragher. New Haven and London: Yale University Press, 1979.

Patchwork of the Past by Mary Eloise Turner (churn dash diagram). Used by permission from Shenandoah Natural History Association.

National Frontier Trails Center, Independence, Missouri.

Daughters of Copper Woman by Anne Cameron ©1981, Press Gang Publishers, Vancouver, BC.

Permission has been granted to publish photographs by the author at the following locations:

National Frontier Trails Center, Independence, Missouri

End of the Oregon Trail Museum, Oregon City, Oregon

"Janus Head" published with permission of Maryhill Museum of Art, Goldendale, Washington

National Historic Oregon Trail Interpretive Center, Baker City, Oregon

"Pioneer Woman" by Aatto Annala "symbolizes the strength and serenity which survived hardship and toil in strange new country." Used by permission of the Hood River County Historical Museum, Hood River, Oregon.

St. Vincent Hospital, Portland, Oregon

LOCATION OF
SOURCE MATERIAL

Following are the locations of documents briefly quoted in my book, some of which appear in other publications:

Adams, Cecelia Emily McMillen and Parthenia Blank. "Crossing the Plains in 1852." Transactions of The Oregon Pioneer Association (1904), 288–329. Diary. Ms. 1508. Oregon Historical Society. (See Kenneth Holmes, *Covered Wagon Women*, vol. V. for clarification as to author citations.)

Bailey, Harriet Elizabeth Tuctness. Fred Lockley, *Conversations with Pioneer Women*, 147–149. Mike Helm, ed. Eugene, OR: Rainy Day Press, 1981.

Bailey, Marilla R. Washburn. Lockley, 164–169.

Bogart, Nancy M. Hembree Snow. "Reminiscences of a Journey Across the Plains in 1843. . . ." Manuscript Diary. The Huntington Library, San Marino, CA.

Buckingham, Harriet Talcott. Diary. Oregon Historical Society, Portland, OR.

Butler, America Rollins. "Mrs. Butler's 1853 Diary of Rogue River Valley." O. Winthur and R. Goley, eds. *Oregon Historical Quarterly*, XLI, No. 4 (December 1940), 337–366.

Carpenter, Helen. "A Trip Across the Plains in an Ox Wagon, 1857." Manuscript Diary. The Huntington Library, San Marino, CA.

Cooke, Lucy Rutledge. *Crossing the Plains in 1852*. Modesto, CA, 1923. Bancroft Library, University of California, Berkeley.

D'Arcy, Marianne Hunsaker Edwards. Lockley, 282–293.

Deady, Lucy Ann Henderson. Lockley, 81–101.

Frizzell, Lodisa. *Across the Plains to California in 1852*. Victor H. Palsits, ed. NY: New York Public Library, 1915.

Hadley, Amelia. Corvallis Public Library, Corvallis, OR

Haun, Catherine. "A Woman's Trip Across the Plains, 1849." Manuscript Diary. The Huntington Library, San Marino, CA.

Hines, Celinda. "Diary, 1853." Transactions of The Oregon Pioneer Association, 1918, 69–125.

Kellogg, Jane D. "Memories, 1852." Transactions of The Oregon Pioneer Association, 1913, 86–94.

Lockhart, Esther M. *Destination West!* The reminiscences of Esther M. Lockhart, told to her daughter, Agnes Ruth Lockhart Sengstacken. Portland, OR: Binfords & Mort, 1942, 35–67.

Markham, Elizabeth. "Poems of Elizabeth Markham," in "The Diary of Elizabeth Dixon Smith." Kenneth L. Holmes, *Covered Wagon Women*, Vol. I. Glendale, CA: Arthur H. Clark Company, 1983, 155.

Masterson, Martha Gay. *One Woman's West.* Lois Barton, ed. Eugene, OR: Spencer Butte Press, 1986.

Owens, Sarah Damron. "Sarah Damron Adair [should be Owens], Pioneer of 1843." Owens-Adair, Dr. [Bethenia], Oregon Pioneer Transactions, 1900, 65–82.

Pengra, Charlotte. Emily Stearns. "Diary, 1853." Eugene, OR: Lane County Historical Society, 1966.

Porter, Lavinia Honeyman. *By Ox Team to California: Narrative of Crossing the Plains in 1860.* Oakland, CA: Oakland Enquirer Publishing Company, 1910.

Smith, Ellen. "A Brief Sketch and History of an Oregon Pioneer, 1846," told by her daughter, Algeline Smith Crews. Manuscript Diary. The Huntington Library, San Marino, CA.

Tuller, Miriam A. Thompson. "Crossing the Plains in 1845." Transactions of The Oregon Pioneer Association, 1895, 87–90.

Whitman, Narcissa. Journal. "The coming of the white women, 1836, as told in the letters, diaries and journals of Narcissa Prentiss Whitman." T.C. Elliott, ed. Oregon Historical Society, Portland, OR.

Williams, Lucia Loraine. Letter to her mother, September 16, 1851. Mrs. Helen Stratton Felker.

Wilson, Margaret Hereford to her mother, Esther Sales, 1850. Manuscript Collection. The Huntington Library, San Marino, CA.

Wood, Elizabeth. "Journal of a Trip to Oregon, 1851." *Oregon Historical Quarterly*, March 1926, 192–203.

END NOTES

Prelude:
1. Quoted in Schlissel, p. 28.
2. Quoted in Schlissel, p. 43.
3. Agnes Stewart, 1853.

Chapter One:
1. *Oregon Blue Book*, p. 432.

Chapter Two:
1. Lomax, p. 124.
2. Quoted in Stoeltje, p. 35.
3. Turner, p. 32.
4. Quoted in Lippard, p. 32.
5. Quoted in Bank, p. 121.
6. Quoted in Barbour, p. 201.
7. Quoted in Dewhurst, MacDowell and MacDowell, p. 99.
8. Quoted in Duffy, p. 8.
9. Turner, p. 37.
10. Welter, p. 106.
11. Quoted in Faragher, p. 94.

Chapter Three:
1. Quoted in Faragher, p. 15.
2. Quoted in Lomax, p. xvii.
3. Ferrero, Hedges and Silber, p. 72.
4. Quoted in Barton, p. 27.
5. Quoted in Jeffrey, p. 37.

Chapter Four:
1. Quoted in Lingenfelter, p. 40.
2. Quoted in Schlissel, p. 78.
3. Quoted in Watson, p. 29.
4. Quoted in Holmes, vol. V, p. 47.
5. Quoted in Myres, p. 106.
6. Quoted in Holmes, vol. III, p. 47.
7. Quoted in Holmes, vol. V, p. 260.
8. Quoted in Schlissel, p. 105.
9. Quoted in Holmes, vol. III, p. 153.
10. Quoted in Holmes, vol. V, p. 130.

Chapter Five:
1. Quoted in McKnight, p. 31-32.
2. Quoted in Schlissel, p. 35.
3. Quoted in Schlissel, p. 43.

4. Quoted in Myres, p. 128.
5. Quoted in Faragher, p. 96.
6. Quoted in Jeffrey, p. 41.
7. Quoted in Holmes, vol. III, p. 156.
8. Quoted in Schlissel, p. 183.
9. Quoted in Alan Lomax, p. 328.
10. Quoted in Holmes, vol. III, p. 166.
11. Watson, p. 29.
12. Quoted in Holmes, vol. III, p. 59.
13. Quoted in Barton, p. 37.
14. Quoted in Schlissel, p. 72.
15. Cited in Holmes, p. 133.
16. Quoted in Faragher, p. 175.
17. Smith, p. 192.
18. Quoted in Holmes, vol. I, p. 155.
19. Quoted in Holmes, vol. III, p. 147.

Chapter Six:
1. Quoted in Lockley, p. 167.
2. Leonore Gale Barette, quoted in Ferrero et al, p. 55.
3. Quoted in Toelken, p. 39.
4. Quoted in Lockley, p. 169.
5. Applegate, p. 108.
6. Gatke, p. 272.
7. Adapted from Gedney, p. 24.
8. Told in Smith, p. 54.
9. Adapted from Gedney, p. 31.
10. King, p. 83.
11. Owens-Adair, p. 75.
12. Told in Smith, p. 117.
13. Quoted in Lockley, p. 149.
14. Owens-Adair, p. 80.

Nebraska:
1. Hickok.
2. Sherr and Kazickas, p. 142.
3. James, vol. II, p. 645.
4. Hickok.

Wyoming:
1. Sumner, p. 50.

Oregon:
1. Quoted in Toelken, p. 37.
2. Quoted in Beckham, p. 32.
3. Craig Lesley, p. 179. Reprinted by permission of author.
4. Quoted in Gunn-Allen, p. 221.

BIBLIOGRAPHY

Allen, John W. *Legends and Lore of Southern Illinois.* Carbondale: Area Services Division, Southern Illinois University, 1963.

Allen, Paula Gunn. *The Sacred Hoop: Recovering the Feminine in American Indian Traditions.* Boston: Beacon Press, 1986.

American History Illustrated. *The Lewis and Clark Expedition.* Gettysburg, PA: The National Historical Society, 1970.

Anderson, C. LeRoy. *Joseph Morris and the Saga of the Morrisites.* Utah State University Press, 1988.

Applegate, Shannon. *Skookum: An Oregon Pioneer Family's History and Lore.* New York: Beech Tree Books/William Morrow, 1988.

Armitage, Susan and Elizabeth Jameson, ed. *The Women's West.* Norman and London: The University of Oklahoma Press, 1987.

Bank, Mirra. *Anonymous Was a Woman.* NY: St. Martin's Press, 1979.

Barnard, Lula, Faunda Bybee and Lola Walker. *Tosoiba.* "Connor's Fort." Soda Springs, ID: Daughters of Utah Pioneers, 1958.

Barbour, Frances M. ed. *Proverbs and Proverbial Phrases of Illinois.* Carbondale: Southern Illinois University Press, 1965.

Barton, Lois, ed. *One Woman's West: Recollections of the Oregon Trail and Settling the Northwest Country by Martha Gay Masterson 1838–1916.* Eugene, OR: Spencer Butte Press, 1986.

Baun, Carolyn M. and Richard Lewis, eds. "Traditional Lifeways": "The Oregon Coast" by Stephen Dow Beckham, "The Plateau Area" by Eugene Hunn, and "The Great Basin" by C. Melvin Aikens and Marilyn Couture. *The First Oregonians.* Portland, OR: Oregon Council for the Humanities, 1991.

Beckham, Stephen Dow. *The Grande Ronde Valley and Blue Mountains: Impressions and Experiences of Travelers and Emigrants, The Oregon Trail, 1812–1880.* Lake Oswego, OR: Beckham and Associates, 1991.

Blood-Patterson, Peter, ed. *Rise Up Singing.* Bethlehem, PA: Sing Out Corporation, 1988.

Bromberg, Erik. "Frontier Humor: Plain & Fancy." *Oregon Historical Quarterly,* LXI (September 1960), 306–317.

Brown, Terry. "An Emigrants' Guide for Women." *American West* (September 1970), 13–17+.

Bullard, William C. *Bound for the Promised Land.* Independence, MO: National Frontier Trails Center, 1990.

——————. Interview, October 12, 1991.

Butruille, Susan G. and Judy Henderson. "Magical History Tour." *The Oregonian,* April 2, 1991, p. C1+.

Butruille, Susan G. and Anita Taylor. "Women in American Popular Song." *Communication, Gender, and Sex Roles in Diverse Interaction Contexts.* Lea Stewart and Stella Ting-Tommey, ed. Norwood, NY: Ablex Publishing, 1987.

Cameron, Anne. *Daughters of Copper Woman*. Vancouver, BC: Press Gang Publishers, 1981.

Carpenter, Harold R., ed. "The Oregon Trail Diary of Amelia Stewart Knight." *Clark County History*, VI (1965), 36–56.

Clark, Ella E. "Indian Thanksgiving in the Pacific Northwest." *Oregon Historical Quarterly*, LXI, No. 4 (December 1960), 444–447.

Cockle, Richard. "Pioneers Found Hardships in Timber Country." *The Oregonian*, August 9, 1992, p. E6.

Dewhurst, C. Kurt, Betty MacDowell and Marsha MacDowell. *Artists in Aprons*. NY: E.P. Dutton, 1979.

Duffy, John. "Medicine in the West: An Historical Overview." *Journal of the West* (July 1982), 5–14.

Duncan, Ruby. Ballads & Folk Songs Collected in Northern Hamilton County. Thesis, University of Tennessee, n.d.

Duniway, Abigail Scott. *Path Breaking: An Autobiographical History of the Equal Suffrage Movement in Pacific Coast States*. NY: Source Book Press, 1914. Second Edition Portland, OR: James, Kerns & Abbott Co., 1970.

Eisler, Riane. *The Chalice and the Blade: Our History, Our Future*. NY: Harper & Row, 1987.

Elliott, T.C. ed. "The coming of the white women, 1836, as told in the letters, diaries and journals of Narcissa Prentiss Whitman." Portland, OR: Oregon Historical Society, 1937.

Enders, Pat McMartin. *Pioneer Woman* (a long poem). San Luis Obispo, CA: Solo Press, 1979.

Evans, Sara M. *Born for Liberty: A History of Women in America*. NY and London: The Free Press, 1989.

Faragher, John Mack. *Women and Men on the Overland Trail*. New Haven and London: Yale University Press, 1979.

Ferrero, Pat, Elaine Hedges and Julie Silber. *Hearts and Hands: The Influence of Women & Quilts on American Society*. San Francisco: The Quilt Digest Press, 1987.

Fitzpatrick, Lilian L. *Nebraska Place-Names*. Lincoln: University of Nebraska Press, 1960.

Franzwa, Gregory M. *The Oregon Trail Revisited* (4th ed.). St. Louis: The Patrice Press, 1988.

_____ . *Maps of the Oregon Trail* (3d ed.). St. Louis: The Patrice Press, 1990.

Friedman, Ralph. *Tracking Down Oregon*. Caldwell, ID: The Caxton Printers, 1978.

Gatke, Robert Moulton, ed. "Ketturah Belknap's Chronicle of the Bellfountain Settlement." *Oregon Historical Quarterly*, XXXVIII (September 1937), 265–299.

Gedney, Elizabeth. "Cross Section of Pioneer Life at Fourth Plain." *Oregon Historical Quarterly*, XLIII (March-December 1942), 14–36.

Gillenwater, Beth. "Pioneer Recipes in a Bountiful Land." *Oregon Journal* (May 29, 1974), 2M, 1.

Gimbutas, Marija. *Civilization of the Goddess: The World of Old Europe*. San Francisco: Harper, 1991.

Godey's Lady's Book and Magazine, vol. LIV (1857), p. 474.

Goltra, Elizabeth. The Oregon Trail Diary of Elizabeth Goltra. Typed by Alice Pitney Norris and Lois Williams. Oregon City, OR, 1988. Unpublished.

Gorge Discoveries: Newsletter of the Gorge Discovery Center, 1, No. 2 (Fall 1991), p. 1–2.

Griswold, Robert L. "Anglo Women and Domestic Ideology in the American West in the Nineteenth and Early Twentieth Centuries." *Western Women: Their Land, Their Lives*. Schlissel et al., ed. Albuquerque, NM: University of New Mexico Press, 1988.

Gulick, Bill. *Roadside History of Oregon*. Missoula: Mountain Press, 1991.

Haines, Aubrey L. *Historic Sites Along the Oregon Trail*. St. Louis: The Patrice Press, 1981.

Hamilton, Mrs. S. Watson. "Pioneer of Fifty-three." *Poems of the Covered Wagons*. Alfred Powers, ed. Portland, OR: Pacific Publishing House, 1947.

Hastings, Lansford W. *The Emigrants Guide to Oregon and California*. Cincinnati: George Conclin, 1845.

Hayes, Susan E. "Crossing the Plains." *Centennial Pioneer Families of Baker County*. Ruth H. Evans, n.d.

Herr, Pamela. "Jessie Benton Fremont: The Story of a Remarkable Nineteenth-Century Woman." *The American West*, XVI, 2 (March/April 1979), 4–13+.

Hickok, Jane Cannary. *Calamity Jane's Letters to Her Daughter*. San Lorenzo, CA: Shameless Hussy Press, 1976.

Historic Preservation League of Oregon. *Oregon Routes of Exploration* (map and text), 1991.

Holden, Jan. "Mother Joseph, Northwest Builder." *Northwest Travel* (April/May 1991), 36–38).

Holmes, Kenneth L., ed. *Covered Wagon Women: Diaries and Letters from the Western Trails, 1840–1890*, Vol. I-IX. Glendale, CA: Arthur H. Clark, 1983–1990.

Huettl, Irene. *Esther Morris of Old South Pass & Other Poems of the West*. Francestown, New Hampshire: The Golden Quill Press, 1965.

Hussey, John A. "The Women of Fort Vancouver." *Oregon Historical Quarterly*, 92, No. 1 (1991), 265–308.

Huyck, Heather. "Beyond John Wayne: Using Historic Sites to Interpret Western Women's History." *Western Women: Their Land, Their Lives*. Schlissel et al., ed. Albuquerque: University of New Mexico Press, 1988.

Hymowitz, Carol and Michaele Weissman. *A History of Women in America*. NY: Bantam, 1978.

Idaho Historical Society. "Three Island Crossing." Reference Series Number 185. Revised 1987.

Idaho Transportation Department. *Idaho Highway Historical Marker Guide* n.d.

Ives, Burl. *Burl Ives Song Book*. New York: Ballantine, 1953.

James, Edward T., ed. *Notable American Women: A Biographical Dictionary*, Vol. I-III. Belknap Press, 1971. Fourth printing, 1975.

Jameson, Elizabeth. "Women as Workers, Women as Civilizers: True Womanhood in the American West." *The Women's West*. Susan Armitage and Elizabeth Jameson, ed. Norman and London: The

University of Oklahoma Press, 1987.

Jeffrey, Julie Roy. *Frontier Women: The Trans-Mississippi West, 1840-1880.* New York: Hill and Wang, 1979.

Johnson, Phillip. *American Women: An Educator's Guide to Documentary Drama.* Jane VanBoskirk on Tour. Oregon Educational Media Association, 1986.

Jones, Suzi. *Oregon Folklore.* Eugene, OR: University of Oregon and the Oregon Arts Commission, 1977.

Kesselman, Amy. Diaries and Reminiscences of Women on the Oregon Trail: A Study in Consciousness. Thesis Portland State University, 1974.

Kessler, Lauren. "A Siege of the Citadels: Search for a Public Forum for the Ideas of Oregon Woman Suffrage." LXXXIV, 2 (Summer 1983), 130-133.

Kimball, Stanley. *Historic Resource Study Mormon Pioneer National Historic Trail.* U.S. Department of the Interior/National Park Service, 1991.

King, Charles R. "The Woman's Experience of Childbirth on the Western Frontier." *Journal of the West* (July 1982), 76-84.

Knight, Amelia Stewart. "Diary of an Oregon Pioneer of 1853." Transactions of The Oregon Pioneer Association, 1928, 38-56.

Lavin, John A. and James A. McGregor. "Native American Childbirth on the Western Plains." University of Colorado Health Sciences Center, n.d. Unpublished.

Leisy, James. *The Good Times Songbook.* Abingdon Press, 1974.

Lesley, Craig. *Winterkill.* Boston: Houghton Mifflin, 1984.

Lingenfelter, Richard E., Richard A. Dwyer and David Cohen. *Songs of the American West.* University of California Press, 1968.

Lippard, Lucy R. "Up, Down, and Across: A New Frame for New Quilts." *The Artist & the Quilt.* Charlotte Robinson, ed. NY: Alfred A. Knopf, 1983.

Lockley, Fred. *Conversations with Pioneer Women.* Mike Helm, ed. Eugene, OR: Rainy Day Press, 1981.

—————. *History of the Columbia River Valley.* Vol. I. Chicago: S. J. Clarke, 1928.

Lomax, Alan. *The Folk Songs of North America.* NY: Doubleday, 1960. Dolphin, 1975.

Lomax, John A. and Alan. *Folk Song USA.* NY: Duell, Sloan and Pearce, 1947.

Luchetti, Cathy and Carol Olwell. *Women of the West.* St. George, Utah: Antelope Island Press, 1982.

Mathes, Valerie Sherer. "Native American Women in Medicine and the Military." *American Folk Medicine: A Symposium.* Hand, Wayland D., ed. University of California Press, 1976.

Mattes, Merrill J. *The Great Platte River Road.* Nebraska State Historical Society, 1969.

—————. *Platte River Road Narratives.* Urbana: University of Illinois Press, 1988.

Maynard, Jane. Diary, 1867, Box 3, Folder 12, MS 590, Katherine Tyler Hunt Collection, Idaho State Historical Society.

McArthur, Harriet Nesmith. "Recollections of the Rickreall." *Oregon*

Historical Quarterly, XXX (March-December 1929), 367–376.

McCarthy, Bridget Beattie. *Where to Find Oregon in Oregon.* Portland, OR: Bridget Beattie McCarthy, 1990.

McKnight, Jeannie. "American Dream, Nightmare Underside: Diaries, Letters, and Fiction of Women on the American Frontier." *Women, Western Writers & the West.* L.L. Lee and Merrill Lewes. Troy, NY: Whitston, 1980.

Menafee, Leah Collins and Lowell Tiller. "Cutoff Fever, III." *Oregon Historical Quarterly,* LXXVIII (June 1977), 121–157.

The Methodist Hymnal. The Methodist Publishing House, 1939.

Moynihan, Ruth Barnes. *Rebel for Rights: Abigail Scott Duniway.* New Haven and London: Yale University Press, 1983.

Myres, Sandra L. *Westering Women and the Frontier Experience, 1800–1915.* Albuquerque: University of New Mexico Press, 1982.

National Park Service. *Fort Laramie: Official Map and Guide.* n.d.

—————. *Fort Vancouver* (brochure). n.d.

Neely, Charles, collected by. *Tales & Songs of Southern Illinois.* Menasha, WI: George Banta Publishing Company, 1938.

Niethammer, Carolyn. *Daughters of the Earth: The Lives and Legends of American Indian Women.* NY: Collier Books, 1977.

Oregon Bluebook. Salem: Office of Secretary of the State, 1989.

Oregon Trail Self Guided Tour. Salem, OR: Oregon State Tourism Offices and Oregon Trail Coordinating Council. n.d.

Oregon Routes of Exploration (map). Historic Preservation League of Oregon, 1991.

Owens-Adair, Dr. [Bethenia]. "Sarah Damron Adair [should be Owens], Pioneer of 1843." Oregon Pioneer Transactions, 1900, 65–82.

Paden, Irene D. *The Wake of the Prairie Schooner.* Southern Illinois University Press, 1943.

Penson-Ward, Betty. *Idaho Women in History.* Boise, Idaho: Legendary Publishing, 1991.

Riley, Glenda. *Women and Indians on the Frontier, 1825–1915.* Albuquerque: University of New Mexico Press, 1984.

Rupp, Virgil. *Let 'Er Buck! A History of the Pendleton Round-Up.* Pendleton, OR: Pendleton Round-Up Association, 1985.

Ruth, Kent. *Landmarks of the West: A Guide to Historic Sites.* Lincoln: University of Nebraska Press, 1986.

Ryan, Mary P. *Womanhood in America From Colonial Times to the Present.* NY: New Viewpoints, 1975.

Sammis, Laurie. "Springs Eternal." *Oh! Idaho: The Idaho State Magazine.* Autumn 1991, pp. 51–55+.

Schlissel, Lillian. "Family on the Western Frontier." *Western Women: Their Land, Their Lives.* Schlissel et al., ed. Albuquerque: University of New Mexico Press, 1988.

—————. Interview. March 10, 1992.

—————. *Women's Diaries of the Westward Journey.* NY: Schocken Books, 1982.

Schlissel, Lillian, Byrd Gibbens and Elizabeth Hampsten. *Far From Home: Families of the Westward Journey.* NY: Schocken Books, 1989.

Schlissel, Lillian, Vicki L. Ruiz and Janice Monk. *Western Women: Their Land, Their Lives.* Albuquerque: University of New Mexico Press, 1988.

Sherr, Lynn and Jurate Kazickas. *The American Woman's Gazetteer.* NY: Bantam, 1976.

Smith, Helen Krebs. *With Her Own Wings.* Portland, OR: Beattie and Company, 1948.

Steber, Rick. *Women of the West.* Prineville, OR: Bonanza Publications, 1988.

Stewart, Agnes. *The Diary of Agnes Stewart, 1853.* Eugene, OR: Lane County Historical Society. Second Printing, 1966.

Stewart, George R. *Ordeal by Hunger: The Classic Story of the Donner Party.* New York: Houghton Mifflin, 1960.

Stewart, Helen. *Diary of Helen Stewart, 1853.* Eugene, OR: Lane County Pioneer Historical Societty. Reproduced 1961.

Stoeltje, Beverly J. "A Helpmate for Man Indeed." *Journal of American Folklore*, 88 (1975), 25–41.

Stone, Merlin. *When God Was a Woman.* NY: Harcourt Brace Jovanovich, 1976.

Story of the Great American West. Pleasantville, NY: The Reader's Digest Association, 1977.

Strong, Emory. *Stone Age on the Columbia River.* Binford & Mort, 1959. 2nd ed., 1982.

Sumner, David. *Wyoming: Upon the Great Plains.* Denver: Sanborn Souvenir Company, 1977.

Tawa, Nicholas E. "The Ways of Love in the Mid-Nineteenth-Century American Song." *Journal of Popular Culture*, 10 (1976), 337–351.

Tinling, Marion. *Women Remembered: A Guide to Landmarks of Women's History in the United States.* NY: Greenwood Press, 1986.

Toelken, Barre. "Northwest Regional Folklore." *Northwest Perspectives: Essays on the Culture of the Pacific Northwest.* Edwin R. Bingham and Glan A. Love, ed. Eugene: University Of Oregon. Seattle and London: University of Washington Press, 1979.

Tompkins, Jim, ed. A.H. Garrison Journal. Oregon Historical Society, 1992. (unpublished)

Tompkins, Jim. The Road to Oregon: Articles About the Oregon Trail. Beavercreek, OR: 1991. (unpublished)

Troxel, Kathryn. "Food of the Overland Emigrants." *Oregon Historical Quarterly* 56, No. 1 (March 1955), 12–26.

Turner, Mary Eloise. *Patchwork of the Past.* Shenandoah Natural History Association, 1976.

US Department of the Interior, Bureau of Land Management. *Oregon Trail in Idaho.* Map and brochure. n.d.

US Department of the Interior, National Park Service. *The Overland Migrations: Settlers to Oregon, California, and Utah.* Washington, DC: GPO, 1980.

—————. *Nez Perce Country.* Washington, DC: Division of Publications, 1983.

USDA Forest Service, Mt. Hood National Forest. *The Barlow Road: Historic Oregon Trail* (map and text). n.d.

Vogel, Virgil J. "American Indian Foods Used as Medicine." *American Folk Medicine: A Symposium*. Wayland D. Hand, ed. University of California Press, 1976.

Walker, Barbara G. *The Woman's Encyclopedia of Myths and Secrets*. NY: Harper and Row, 1983.

Watson, Jeanne H. "Women's Travails and Triumphs on the Overland Trails." *Overland Journal* 9, No. 4 (Winter 1991), 28–36.

Welter, Barbara. "The Cult of True Womanhood, 1820–1860." *American Quarterly* (Summer 1966, Part 1), 151–174.

Wenner, Hilda E. and Elizabeth Freilicher. *Here's to the Women*. Syracuse University Press, 1987.

Wertheimer, Barbara Mayer. *We Were There: The Story of Working Women in America*. NY: Pantheon Books, 1977.

Wolford, Leah Jackson. *The Play-Party in Indiana*. Indianapolis: Indiana Historical Society, 1959.

Wojcik, Donna M. *The Brazen Overlanders of 1845*. Portland, OR: Donna M. Wojcik, 1976.

Wright, Merideth. *Put on Thy Beautiful Garments: Rural New England Clothing, 1783–1800*. East Montpelier, VT: The Clothes Press, 1990.

Wynne, Patrice. "Recovering Spiritual Reality in Native American Traditions: An Interview with Paula Gunn Allen." *Woman of Power*, 8 (Winter 1988), p. 68–70.

Wyoming Recreation Commission. *Wyoming: A Guide to Historic Sites*. Basin, Wyoming: Big Horn Publishers, 1988.

Wyoming Division of Tourism and The Wagner Perspective. *Wagons Across Wyoming: Oregon Trail 150 Years* (map and brochure). Cheyenne: Wyoming Division of Tourism, 1992.

Yakima Nation Museum. Fact Sheet. Yakima Nation Cultural Center, Toppenish, Washington.

INDEX

The author welcomes comments and suggestions for subsequent editions of *Women's Voices from the Oregon Trail*. Please write c/o Tamarack Books, PO Box 190313, Boise, ID 83719-0313.

Additional copies of *Women's Voices from the Oregon Trail* can be found in fine bookstores everywhere or directly from the publisher.

If ordering direct, please include a check for $17.45 (book @ $14.95 plus a shipping/handling charge of $2.50). Idaho residents should send $18.33 (book @ 14.95, shipping/handling $2.50, and Idaho tax .88).

Send your name, address, and check to:

Orders
Tamarack Books, Inc.
PO Box 190313
Boise, ID 83719-0313

To place orders using MasterCard or Visa, please call 1-800-962-6657.

The author and her mother, Ruth Greffenius, at the Whitman Mission National Historic Site near Walla Walla, Washington.

Photo by Kay Koller

ABOUT THE AUTHOR

Susan G. Butruille's writing career began with a fishing column for an Alaskan newspaper. Since then, she has published widely in newspapers and magazines and edited publications for The Council of American Embroiderers and The National Association for Training and Development. A member of the speaker's bureau for the California-based Center for Partnership Studies, she is a seasoned keynote speaker and workshop presenter.

16 $\frac{2}{0}$ $\frac{3}{2}$

1844 OR exclusion Act
1837 Depression & 49

21 new plow 1850;
36 good cooking — good friends

Barbara Welter — cult of True womanhood